CAIRO PAPERS IN SOCIAL SCIENCE
VOLUME 35   NUMBER 1

Oral History in Times of Change
Gender, Documentation, and the Making of Archives

Edited by
Hoda Elsadda
Hanan Sabea

Contributors
Faiha Abdulhadi   Sondra Hale
Manal Hamzeh   Maissan Hassan
Nahawand El Kaderi Issa   Diana Magdy
Jean Said Makdisi   Noor Nieftagodien
Rafif Saidawy   Lucine Taminian
Stephen Urgola

THE AMERICAN UNIVERSITY IN CAIRO PRESS
CAIRO   NEW YORK

Cover photo: courtesy of Farah Shoukry

This paperback edition first published in 2023 by
The American University in Cairo Press
113 Sharia Kasr el Aini, Cairo, Egypt
420 Lexington Avenue, Suite 1644, New York, NY 10170
www.aucpress.com

First published in an electronic edition in 2018

Copyright © 2018, 2023 by the American University in Cairo Press

All rights reserved. No part of this publication may be reproduced, stored in a retrieval system, or transmitted in any form or by any means, electronic, mechanical, photocopying, recording, or otherwise, without the prior written permission of the publisher.

ISBN 978 1 649 03235 5

Library of Congress Cataloging-in-Publication Data applied for

1 2 3 4 5   27 26 25 24

Designed by Adam el-Sehemy

Contents

1 Introduction 1
  Hoda Elsadda and Hanan Sabea

Part One
Times of Change: Redrawing Boundaries
of Knowledge, Memory, and History 13

2 Recuperating Women's Memory as Knowledge:
  Sudan's Conflict Zones 14
  Sondra Hale

3 Women's Activism and Contending Narratives of
  Liberation in South Africa 29
  Noor Nieftagodien

4 The Production of Alternative Knowledge: Political Participation
  of Palestinian Women since the 1930s: A Case Study 45
  Faiha Abdulhadi

Part Two
Intersections: Alternative Fields of History 62

5 Memory, Memoir and Oral History 63
  Jean Said Makdisi

6   The Novel as a Repository for Oral and Women's History   77
    Rafif Saidawy

7   Palestinian Memory in Light of New Technology:
    Opportunities and Challenges   94
    Nahawand El Kaderi Issa

Part Three
Ethical and Methodological Questions   112

8   Documenting the Oral History of Iraqis in Times of Conflict:
    Challenges, Ethics, and Standards of Practice   113
    Lucine Taminian

9   *Testimonio* as Methodology: Archiving, Translating, and
    Theorizing Egyptian Women's Experiences of Gendered
    Violence in the January 25th Revolution   124
    Manal Hamzeh

Part Four
Praxis: Entanglements in Two Projects Documenting
Gender and Revolution   133

10 Narrating Gender in Egypt's Public Sphere:
    The Archive of Women's Oral History   134
    Maissan Hassan and Diana Magdy

11 University on the Square: Documenting Egypt's
    21st-Century Revolution Project   145
    Stephen Urgola

    About the Contributors   153

CHAPTER 1
Introduction

Hoda Elsadda and Hanan Sabea

In the 1960s, oral history projects were at the forefront of liberatory social movements in general, and the feminist movement in particular. Feminist historians challenged mainstream historical narratives that fed normalized cultural stereotypes of women's roles in history and society: they documented the marginalized voices of women and integrated their diverse points of view in historical narratives; they engaged in intellectual debates about the relation between the social and the individual, the workings of memory and the construction of subjectivity, and the relation between personal memory and collective memory. They also played a key role in highlighting the value of subjectivity and subverting the pseudo-binary between subjective and objective histories. In short, feminist oral historians succeeded in creating a knowledge backbone to support women's movements in many countries in the world by creating archives of women's lives, struggles, and voices. These interventions left their mark on critical engagements with histories of the marginalized and the oppressed whether the locus of study was gender, class, ethnicity, colonialism, or religion, among others. Oral histories, and feminist oral histories in particular, thus had significant implications for emancipatory politics and the forging of solidarities among diverse social movements and the academic debates that unfolded around them (see, for instance, Bonart and Diamond 2007; McEwan 2003; Armitage and Gluck 1998; Green 1997; Nair 2008; Geiger 1986).

Until the end of the twentieth century in the Arab world, archives of women's voices were almost nonexistent, despite the presence of many small documentation efforts tied to individual research projects (see, for instance, Abu-Lughod 1993; Sayigh 1998). However, the twenty-first century witnessed a marked increase in documentation projects in general, and of Arab women's voices in particular. The escalation of violence and exclusion that occasioned neoliberal governmentality, and the corresponding heightening of diverse modes of resistance and struggle against injustices and oppression, prompted many archiving efforts to document moments, events, spaces, and practices of contestation of power. Diverse social groups and movements globally who struggled against dispossession, violence, occupation, and expulsion from normative orders regulated by patriarchal structures of state and capital deployed different technologies and tactics in their search for justice and recognition. Alternative histories and practices of the contemporary became a hallmark not only of academe but, equally important, of ordinary men and women who sought to challenge the hegemony of the written, the archive, and the document as means through which relations to the past and present are articulated. Witnessing, listening, sensing, seeing, and documenting the everyday, the ephemeral, the immaterial, and the not so visible, became critical tools in practicing, relating to, and producing knowledge about domains, agents, spaces, and temporalities that emerged as key actors in making history and remaking the present. In the Arab world, the second intifada in 2000, the war on Iraq in 2003, the invasion of Lebanon in 2006, and most recently, the wave of Arab revolutions in 2011, resulted in radical historical transformations whose meanings continue to be contested and negotiated between the warring factions within academe and diverse communities engaged in processes of radical change. In addition, new technologies (e.g., digital technologies, social media, alternative museums, artistic productions, documentary film, and social theater, among others) brought in new practitioners and new audiences and have transformed the field of oral history, historiography, what comprises an archive, and what passes as "history."

The increase in the radical shifts and upheavals in the Arab body politic poses a range of challenges to oral history practitioners about the role and limits of oral history in times of change. Many questions arise: What are the limits and potentials of oral history projects in times of change? How can oral history enable women to become active participants in transitional politics? What are the challenges facing oral historians/practitioners in an environment marked by bitter political divisions? What becomes of the archive, the document, and the written? What are the dangers of doing oral history in times of radical change? What are the challenges posed by the digital revolution in the field of oral history? What are the challenges to the construction of an 'objective' and 'representative' archive of voices in turbulent times with a gender lens? What are times of change and how should change itself be conceived? How does a sensibility to different simultaneous temporalities challenge the linearity and singularity of time progression that marks the writings of [H]istory or his-tory? What becomes of the political once we move the lens from the victorious to the excluded, from the center to the margins, and from the written to the oral and the sensory? What are the ethics of remembering and forgetting? What are the edges of the stories deployed in the struggle over the truth claims, legitimacy, and legibility of different pasts?

The conference "Oral History in Times of Change: Gender, Documentation and the Making of Archives," organized by the Women and Memory Forum, in cooperation with the Supreme Council of Culture in Egypt and held in Cairo on September 13–15, 2015 brought together scholars, researchers, students, artists, and practitioners to exchange views and experiences regarding the challenges facing oral history projects in times of change, with a particular focus on gender. The conference focused on documentation initiatives in Arab countries in transitional and conflict situations but also explored international experiences, particularly the South African contribution to the field of oral history in the post-apartheid era.

Over three days, participants in the conference discussed and deliberated questions and concerns around archives as a manifestation of power, the challenges and opportunities presented by new technologies to the making and preserving of archives, ethical concerns in the construction of archives, women's archives, and the production of alternative knowledge, as well as conceptual and methodological issues in oral history. Participants also explored the intersections and fluid boundaries between oral narratives, memoirs, autobiographies, biographies, social media, and novels, various generic expressions that cross the boundaries of the personal to the public and the collective. Memories and histories were subject to critical rethinking as informed by the many debates that occasioned the radical emergence of memory and memory studies in academe and beyond. The fluidity, malleability, and subjectivity that once marked the domain of memory were placed in relation to history, opening up the space for revisiting the blurred boundaries between the two. How power, silences, and refusals mark the production of histories was a common thread connecting the conversations at the conference.

The idea of the conference came as a response to the many questions and issues that confronted the WMF research team working on the creation of an oral history archive of women. The first phase of the WMF Oral History Project began at the end of the 1990s and focused on collecting life stories of Egyptian women who were not famous but had played a role in public life as professionals, founders and members of charity organizations, and many other contributions. The second phase of the WMF project was inspired by the revolutionary moment in 2011, when women were recognized as key participants in the movements for change but were nevertheless marginalized in formal political processes. We feared a repeat of the same old story: that women will again be marginalized and silenced in the official mainstream history, the meta-narrative about the events, and what constituted the event of change. We have seen this happen in Algeria, where women were freedom fighters at the forefront of the struggle for liberation, were asked to postpone their demands for equality until after the struggle against colonialism was won, and then found themselves abandoned and marginalized by their comrades. We have seen this happen in many histories. Noor Nieftagodien sheds light in his paper on the marginalization of South African women in the anti-apartheid master narrative where women were represented as mothers, supporters, and helpers, disregarding their role in direct confrontational struggles. Faiha Abdulhadi's contribution in this volume also addresses the continued struggle of Palestinian women, which many a time goes unrecognized or remains confined to the domain of the domestic. Sondra Hale's paper takes us to Sudan, where she hails "memory work" as a critical site for the production of different knowledges and politics.

In addition to the known challenge of women's marginalization in historical narratives, we were also concerned about another pressing challenge, the challenge of conflicting narratives in times of change.

Introduction 5

Narratives of Arab revolutions are typically diverse and conflicting: they are sites of contestation. Questions range from what happened and who was responsible, to whether it happened at all. Was this a revolution, a protest movement, a "refolution" as Asef Bayat (2013) called it? Was it a soft military coup? Is it ongoing? Has it ended? What is remarkable and worthy of consideration is that these contesting narratives exist against the background of a moment in history that has seen almost unprecedented media coverage and interest. The Egyptian revolution in particular has been described as "Revolution 2.0" in reference to the new generation of digital media technology that has allowed ordinary citizens to interact and publish accounts, news items, and their own stories about what happened, or rather about their perceptions of events as they occurred. Also, and almost instantly, websites and Facebook pages were created to gather and collect documents, photos, statements, videos, and various news items related to the revolution. Documenting the revolution became a goal for various actors, an endeavor that was enabled by the technological revolution. The challenge remained: did the abundant overflow of information facilitate and enable our understanding of what happened, or did it result in a state of misinformation, or even a situation where powerful media networks maintained their control over the dissemination of information and succeeded in manipulating new technologies in the creation and consolidation of yet another master narrative that was exclusionary and biased towards power? What are the "ethics of forgetting," as Ashis Nandy asks? Who and what has been silenced, and in what form was such silence represented? How to challenge the disjuncture between what happened and what various groups have said has happened? Who owns the archive(s) of the revolution? And what constitutes an archive of the revolution? How to document the affective infrastructure that occasioned such intensive processes of change, and how to accept the incompleteness of the archives of revolutions and their constant transformative, and to no small extent ephemeral, nature?

Recognizing the complexity of such moments and desires for archiving, the Women and Memory Forum decided to embark on the second phase of the oral history archive of women and collect narratives of women about their experiences post-2011: their memories of key moments, their perceptions of what happened and why, their thoughts on how they themselves were affected or changed. The aim is to construct an alternative to the master narrative in the media post-2011. Many questions arose around the implications of an "alternative" archive of women's narratives. What does a gender-sensitive archive that counters the narrative of power look like? How do we avoid the trappings of archives as instruments of power? Archives are necessarily entangled in the construction of hegemonic narratives as well as counter-hegemonic narratives that potentially shape the future of a given group or country. They are inevitably sites of contestation and revisioning. As Constantin Fasolt (2003) argues, such knowledge falls under the rubric of "dangerous knowledge," by virtue of the complexity it reveals or enables, but also the risks it demands. The Women and Memory Oral History Archive of Women is no exception–it is inevitably entangled in the history of struggles over memory. It is deliberately conceived as an intervention in the narrative of and about the revolution. It positions itself within a "politics of hope" in lieu of a "politics of despair" (Elsadda 2016). It celebrates women's agency within a larger narrative of citizen engagement and empowerment and tells a story of possibilities and potential for change. It counters narratives of apathetic and disenfranchised populations. It captures the complex interactions and shifting positions between surrender and perseverance, love and hate, belief and disillusionment.

The overarching theme of the collected essays in this volume revolves around the play of memory, power, gender justice, and the nature of an archive that takes into consideration the challenges and issues at stake. The past two decades have witnessed what has been described as a "memory boom" (Boesen 2012:7) as more and more marginalized groups who have been excluded from mainstream or national archives have focused on the creation of their memories. They tell their stories in a multiplicity of forms and genres—oral testimonies, personal accounts, songs, performances, pictures, videos, graffiti—all in an attempt to counter or revise official narratives. They are the "fragments of history," to use Gyanendra Pandey's words, that express the voice of minorities or marginalized groups in any society and are invariably excluded from official mainstream histories (Pandey 1992:28; see also Hamilton 2002). Some of these diverse forms of expression pose another challenge: the importance of the ephemeral archive in the construction of memory.

Introduction

Archiving the peripheral, the fragmentary, and the ephemeral raises new epistemological questions about what counts as knowledge, what knowledges are worthy of preserving and archiving, who is the knower, and who has the authority to define knowledge. Such archives challenge dominant narratives, give credence and historical value to the voices and points of view of marginalized groups or communities, and consequently subvert pretensions of objectivity and impartiality posited by custodians of archives that claim to safeguard the history of 'the nation' or 'the state.' Indeed, as Mbembe argues, "The power of the archive as an 'instituting imaginary' largely originates in its trade with death . . . the struggle against the fragments of life being dispersed" (2002:22). He adds: "And this is why the historian and the archivist have long been so useful to the state, notably in contexts where the latter was set up as a guardian of that domain of things that belong exclusively to no one" (2002:26). But who owns the past, the archive, and the memories? Can they be owned, and are all accessible in the same way? What about those archives and memories that are not even recognized as an archive, worthy of policing, housing, organizing, and protecting? What other archives can challenge the hegemony of the document, the building, and the monument?

Women's archives, which house women's oral narratives and women's cultural production, have played a key role in shaping women's rights movements and activism in many countries in the world. They tell a story of strength, of agency, and of achievement. They also expose the dynamics of power, the processes of exclusion and marginalization to which women are and have been subjected, and the misogynistic authoritarianism behind the thinking and epistemological paradigms that deem women's experiences and life narratives unworthy of inclusion in mainstream histories. Revealing the silences, the positionality in narrating the past, and the techniques of exclusion in the making of history, as Trouillot (1995) argues, becomes a significant underpinning in excavating different pasts and histories. Writing women's stories, recording women's memories, and unearthing women's hidden knowledge production have all contributed to a revisionist movement in recording various histories and cultural traditions. They also have revealed different structures of feeling, as Stoler claims (2010), that remained subsumed under a logic of the "common-sense" about history, power, and change.

Issues pertaining to archives, gender, and power were the topic of two roundtable discussions in the conference. The first of these, entitled "Archives and Power" and coordinated by Emad Abu Ghazi, highlighted the intricate link between archives and power, particularly in the modern nation-state, on three levels: the production of archival documents; their accessibility, or who controls the narrative; and the credibility of the documents, drawing attention to the importance of a critical scrutiny of official documents to ascertain whose point of view is represented and what other points of view are excluded. The second roundtable, entitled "Feminist Archives and the Production of Alternative Knowledge" and coordinated by Hoda Elsadda, put forward the contention that a feminist archive necessarily problematizes epistemological questions about knowledge: which knowledge is worth knowing and documenting, and who the knower is, with the view of deconstructing patriarchal intellectual hierarchies in knowledge production that have resulted in the marginalization of women's knowledges and experiences. In a feminist archive, the personal is political. It is created with a gender lens, which necessarily foregrounds the interplay between all manifestations of oppression based on gender, race, class, and nationality. It is not exclusive to feminist voices, or women's voices for that matter: rather, it problematizes relations of power and exposes the silences and the blind spots.

Rather than 'documenting' or providing an 'archive' of the conference as a whole, this volume consists of a selection of articles presented, representing four key organizational nodes or sections. Part one, "Times of Change: Redrawing Boundaries of Knowledge, Memory and History," consists of three articles which engage critically with the challenges of conducting oral history in times of change using a gender lens in three very different settings: Sudan, Palestine, and South Africa. Sondra Hale argues that "recuperating memory in times of oppression and war can be a form of resistance," and engages critically with the limits and potential of archiving memories during or after conflict situations. Drawing on her extensive knowledge of Sudanese women's movements, she sheds light on the gendered bio-politics where women's bodies are manipulated as symbols of warring factions over national identity. Women as icons of the nation and national liberation projects are a recurrent theme in post-colonial historical narratives. In Palestine, where occupation continues to

Introduction

be a reality on the ground in the twenty-first century, Faiha Abdulhadi exposes the contradictions in the national narrative which, on the one hand, celebrates women as symbols of national identity, but at the same time undermines their contribution to the national struggle. Through oral history narratives, women are encouraged to share their stories and counter the dominant narratives, which limit their contribution to helpers and mothers and shed light on the role of rural women, for example, in the armed struggle. Similarly, Noor Nieftagodien argues that the post-apartheid narrative of liberation in South Africa focused on the role of the ANC and nation building, and confined women to their traditional roles as "ancillaries in the struggle led by men." Oral history compensated for this gap in the official narrative by shedding light on the role of women as active contributors and leaders of protest movements.

Part two, "Intersections: Alternative Fields of History," explores the diverse forms through which memories and histories are experienced, narrated, and practiced. It also engages debates about the crossing of geographical, disciplinary, and genre boundaries where memories, both personal and public, are interwoven in historical narratives. Focusing on the memoir, Jean Makdisi refutes generic boundaries that consolidate claims of authenticity and credibility of some historical sources over others, and argues that all documents, notes, minutes of official meetings—that is, all the sources of official narratives—are grounded in memory. Writing about narratives of key moments in Palestinian history, she notes that memory "is the heart and soul of the Palestine struggle." From the memoir to the novel, Rafif Saidawy reflects on the social function of memory and remembering. She argues that all novels are historical and that the novelistic tradition represents an archive of social memories. Historical novels play an important role in resisting amnesia, both political and social, and encourage remembrance and revisionist readings of the past, particularly as regards women's histories and gendered roles. New technologies are the third domain this section presents through the work of Nahawand Elkadery Issa, who addresses the manifestations of memory in media venues. She examines social media, blogs, and electronic archives that document and shed light on Palestinian history and resistance to occupation. Her article highlights the radical transformations brought by the technological revolution in enabling ordinary citizens to become oral historians.

Part three, "Ethical and Methodological Questions," raises methodological questions and ethical issues in oral history projects. Lucine Taminian discusses the challenges facing oral historians conducting fieldwork with people who have experienced armed conflict, namely Iraqis in the diaspora. Under stress, the oral historian must take into consideration factors that impact not only the process of interviewing, but also the content and final outcome, such as potential risks to interviewees as a consequence of agreeing to tell their stories, the complex relation between the interviewer and the interviewee and the challenge of building trust, and the perceptions of the interviewee about history and the dominance of official narratives. Manal Hamzeh, on the other hand, makes a case for using the methodology of *testimonio* to enable an understanding of gender-based violence against women post–25 January 2011. She explains that *testimonios* must be distinguished from oral history interviewing, in the sense that they are political statements, which aim to counter injustice. She joins a long tradition of oral history writing that focuses on bearing witness and documenting accounts that can be used as evidence in courts.

Finally, part four, "Praxis: Entanglements in Two Projects Documenting Gender and Revolution," sheds light on two specific oral history projects, or the praxis of oral history in times of change: the American University in Cairo's "University on the Square," described by Stephen Urgola, and the Women and Memory Forum's "Archive of Women's Oral History," discussed by Maissan Hassan and Diana Magdy. Both projects were inspired by the wave of revolutions which engulfed the Arab world in 2011, and both aimed to capture and document the stories and experiences of first-hand witnesses and participants in the events of the Egyptian revolution.

Neither the editors nor the authors contributing to this volume provide fixed answers to the range of questions that are raised. The aim is rather to open the space for alternative practices of relating, practicing, and experiencing knowledge (see Law 2004), of recognizing events and non-events, of revealing fleeting ephemeral experiences, of recognizing the mundane and the ordinary as inseparable from the making of history, and of hailing different actors in the production of the political and of history. The volume invites us also to reimagine the value and ethics of forgetting and remembering, the limits of the 'awe' of the archive and the document, and the magic of the oral, the performative, and the sensory in illuminating domains of knowledge oft hidden, silenced, or excised in thinking about time and temporality.

References

Abu-Lughod, Lila. 1993. *Writing Women's Worlds: Bedouin Stories*. Berkeley: University of California Press.

Armitage, Susan, and Sherna Berger Gluck. 1998. "Reflections on Women's Oral History: An Exchange," *Frontiers: A Journal of Women's Studies*, 19(3): 1–11.

Bayat, Asef. 2013. "Revolution in Bad Times," *New Left Review*, 80, March–April. https://newleftreview.org/II/80/asef-bayat-revolution-in-bad-times.

Boesen, Elisabeth. 2012. "Peripheral Memories–Introduction." In Elisabeth Boesen, Fabienne Lentz, Michel Margue, Denis Scuto, and Renee Wagener, eds. *Peripheral Memories: Public and Private Forms of Experiencing and Narrating the Past*, 7–20. Bielefeld: Transcript Verlag.

Bonart, Joanna, and Hanna Diamond. 2007. "Women's History and Oral History: Developments and Debates," *Women's History Review*, 16(1): 19–39.

Elsadda, Hoda. 2016. "An Archive of Hope: Translating Memories of Revolution." In Mona Baker, ed. *Translating Dissent: Voices from and with the Egyptian Revolution*, 148–60. London: Routledge.

Fasolt, Constantin. 2003. *The Limits of History*. Chicago: University of Chicago Press.

Geiger, Susan. 1986. "Women's Life Histories: Method and Content," *Signs*, 11(2): 334–351.

Green, Anna. 1997. "Returning History to the Community: Oral History in a Museum Setting," *The Oral History Review*, 24(2): 53–72.

Hamilton, Carolyn. 2002. "'Living by Fluidity': Oral Histories, Material Custodies and the Politics of Archiving." In Carolyn Hamilton et al., eds. *Refiguring the Archive*, 209–228. Cape Town: David Philip.

Law, John. 2004. *After Method: Mess in Social Science Research*. New York: Routledge.

Mbembe, Achille. 2002. "The Power of the Archive and Its Limits." In Carolyn Hamilton et al., eds. *Refiguring the Archive*, 19–26. Cape Town: David Philip.

McEwan, Cheryl. 2003. "Building a Postcolonial Archive? Gender, Collective Memory and Citizenship in Post-Apartheid South Africa," *Journal of Southern African Studies*, 29(3): 739–757.
Nair, Janaki. 2008. "The Troubled Relationship of Feminism and History," *Economic and Political Weekly*, October 25.
Nandy, Ashis. 1995. "History's Forgotten Doubles," *History and Theory*, 34 (2): 44–66.
Pandey, Gyanendra. 1992. "In Defense of the Fragment: Writing about Hindu–Muslim Riots in India Today," *Representations*, 37 (Winter): 27–55.
Sayigh, Rosemary. 1998. "Palestinian Camp Women as Tellers of History," *Journal of Palestine Studies*, 27(2): 42–58.
Stoler, Ann. 2010. *Along the Archival Grain: Epistemic Anxieties and Colonial Common Sense*. Princeton: Princeton University Press.
Trouillot, Michel-Rolph. 1995. *Silencing the Past: Power and the Production of History*. New York: Beacon Press.

I

Times of Change: Redrawing Boundaries of Knowledge, Memory, and History

CHAPTER 2

Recuperating Women's Memory as Knowledge: Sudan's Conflict Zones

Sondra Hale

Introduction

In the background of this essay is my consideration of the forms and sources of knowledge—especially unrecognized, subversive, subjugated knowledge—and knowledge as resistance. I consider memory-as-knowledge to contain all of these. My interest within the politics of knowledge is, first, the fact that unrecognized knowledge may be potentially subversive and subjugated knowledge may potentially become a form of resistance, and these are often acts against those who are attempting to control history and politics. Second, I have a stake in the ways in which we can innovate with that knowledge. Third, I have an interest in the ways in which we can transmit that knowledge, for example, through pedagogical strategies that would involve developing methods for bringing knowledge to the surface and then putting that knowledge into action (as Paulo Freire advocated). Fourth, I have been thinking about the ways in which we can form archives and work out methodologies for analyzing repertoires. Clearly I will not be able to discuss all of these processes in one essay, but I am hoping to gesture toward these various themes, even if not directly discussing them.

Let us take the transmission of knowledge as our first example of the complexity of our subject. We can transmit knowledge in very diverse ways: for example, through our technologies; through our arts, media, and culture; through oral histories; through hermeneutics (interpretation of texts), academic writings, propaganda, modeling; through relating our dreams; through silence and body language and other unspoken messages; and through imparting our memories to others. We most conventionally think of the transmission of knowledge as a process of teacher-to-student. However, pedagogy is not only a linear way in which we pass on knowledge or receive it. Something can happen to the knowledge in the process of the transmission; innovation can occur, changing knowledge in the process. Therefore, we have to consider the ways in which we change not only the listener/viewer/student/interrogator, but ourselves in the process, because of what the holder of memories might be giving back, but also because the context itself might be changing. All of these processes make capturing repertoire and archiving memory or memories very complicated, namely this notion that something may happen to the memory in the process of retelling or performing.

I have at least six agendas in dealing specifically with memory-as-knowledge: (1) to validate memory as a significant area of knowledge; (2) to recuperate memory in highly fraught conflict situations, partially to juxtapose the memories of the actors in the conflict to the "official story," and partially to illuminate the memories of women in any of their roles in conflicts; (3) to argue that recuperating memory in times of oppression and war can be a form of resistance; (4) to develop the interpretation of memory and the politics of memory for evidentiary purposes in bringing about transitional justice; (5) to work out how to manage and archive that flood of memory data, either in the midst of conflict or post-conflict; and (6) to figure out how to differentiate between repertoire and archive, or acknowledge the blurring of these lines.

I am researching these themes within the context of Sudan (and the palimpsest of South Sudan), an area that has had more internal (and now external) conflicts than virtually any other North African state. I am considering the entire country as a "conflict zone," even those areas not directly involved, at the moment, in armed struggle. Where women have figured in these conflicts has long concerned me. I am focused on women's memories in Sudanese political struggles as unrecognized, subjugated, and subversive, and the recuperation of those memories as simultaneously a political act and an archive.

I am arguing, therefore, for the use of a particular methodology for interpreting people's ideas that emerge from conflict situations. I am calling it "memory-work"—both the memory-work of those engaged in a conflict or post-conflict situation or the fieldworker's memory-work (i.e., collecting the memories of people involved in conflict)—in this case, mine. In a way, I am advocating offsetting or resisting a type of epistemic imperialism or the application of "expert knowledge" as interventions in crises. This expert knowledge is applied by the state, non-governmental organizations (NGOs), military and paramilitary actors, "traditional authorities" (usually male), and foreign experts and advisors. Memory-work is the process of recuperating memory and processing it as a form of knowledge. In other words, it is knowledge or data retrieval. Assuming that all knowledge is political, the retrieval of this knowledge can be a form of political resistance to those who are attempting to control knowledge—those who are considered the "knowers," the owners of "truth." Therefore, one of the subtext questions of this essay, arguably rhetorical, is whether indigenous or local knowledge/memory is more valid than introduced information with its claims of "objectivity." I cannot avoid, then, the implication that the memory-as-knowledge we collect from women may have added value, if not greater value. By recounting what has happened to them in conflicts—oftentimes through poetic renderings—women may try to override, cancel out, and/or morally supersede their adversaries' renditions. Do memories that are "closer to home," so to speak, even among women guerrillas, have a greater or a different value than those that are articulated either by men or by people trained by men? I do not intend to answer this question, only to raise it.

The Politics of Memory

By the term "the politics of memory," I am referring to the various ways that memory-as-knowledge is arranged and rearranged, for example: the way the memorist may shape the particular memory for the situation (or the way the situation has shaped the memory); the way others are receiving it and acting or not acting on it; the relationship of the memory to the "official story" (the state, scholarly or journalistic accounts, or "expert" testimony); and the way that I, the researcher, am interpreting it for the situation.

To use a variation of the term, in the conflict situations which I am researching, "political memory" is an arena where people confront each other with the past and refute each other's telling of the past. In some conflicts adversaries may try to kill memory, that is, their adversary's idea of his or her past. Likewise, people may try to colonize each other's pasts, appropriating the story and altering it in the process. State policy may be aimed at eliminating, inventing, shaping, or colonizing memory. Agents of state policy have various strategies for these interventions: rupturing time and space; annihilating culture; forcing one group's practices on another; exterminating intellectuals such as historians or organic intellectuals as the carriers of indigenous knowledge; dislocating people from their homeland and/or forcing them to live among different ethnic groups; controlling the flow of knowledge through altering school curricula; and my primary interest—trying to shape/control the lives, bodies, and voices of women.

In various African and Middle Eastern conflict zones not only do different ethnic groups and people with differing modes of economy remember their pasts differently, so do women and men. It is this gender dynamic that I feature in this essay. But I also underscore the ways in which people resist how their knowledge is managed by others. In short, in various Sudanese conflict situations—whether the "heroic life" of the revolutionary or the militarized life—not only do competing ethnic and regional groups, political parties, and people with differing modes of economy remember their encounters differently, so do women and men. During conflict situations, men may try to recapture stories of the "homeland" through the bodies of women, a provocative process that may lead to gender-based violence. By substituting their own poetics and polemics, women and other minoritized groups resist a biopolitics in which their bodies are used as a symbolic means of dramatizing conflicts. Susan Slyomovics, in discussing Palestine, points out that "the ... woman is made to stand for the destroyed villages and the dispossessed land. She represents the 'national allegory' of the lost ... homeland."[1]

Another factor is that so much of the politics of knowledge is related to identity and representation. The past is always contested, but the focus of contestation is not so much about what happened in the past as it is about who or what is entitled to speak for that past in the present (i.e., the gatekeepers of historical knowledge), and this is often a conflict over representation—the question of whose views should be

---

1 Slyomovics 1998:208. Here she is using ideas from Fredric Jameson and Partha Chatterjee.

sought. There could be agreement over events, but not over how the truth of these events may be most fully represented. What enters is the role of memory. Yet both memory and truth are unstable categories.[2]

People everywhere resist the state or "official" history. The 1998 documentary *In Search of Palestine* depicts Edward Said's return to Palestine after 47 years. In the film, he engages in what Slyomovics refers to in her 1998 book, *The Object of Memory*, as the "repeated gesture," which specifically involves pointing to a remembered site (Slyomovics 1998). Many times in the film the viewer sees Said pointing over and over again at a site. The repeated gesture reminds us, reminds him, and marks the landscape. His individual memory contradicts the official memory, creates a history, and reshapes knowledge. We see many repeated gestures and pointing from Sudanese women in conflict zones.

Sudanese Women Bearing Witness and Resisting

Women have been very active and powerful in bearing witness to Sudanese conflicts where oftentimes people are violently driven off their land. We see women actively pointing fingers—either in actuality or metaphorically in speech—at the past and toward the future, as I said, often using the "repeated gesture."[3] A Nuba woman I was interviewing about the violence in the Nuba Mountain area of west-central Sudan was recounting being raped during the Nuba conflict with the Islamist-controlled and "Arab"-identified Sudanese government. All the while she was talking to me she kept pointing to an old colonial-era map of Sudan that was hanging in the starkly furnished room in a women's center in Omdurman. When she was vaguely gesturing toward the Nuba Mountains she used "we," but she used "they" when she gestured toward Khartoum on the map. Or sometimes she would unconsciously (?) point toward a presumed northern Sudanese man we could see who was leaning against the building right outside the window where we were. She was a witness, using the repeated gesture to construct her own history

---

2 I am using ideas from Hodgekin and Radstone 2003.
3 Slyomovics 1998:10–14, especially in chapter 1 when she discusses "Photographing Loss." She says, "What is most important about the pointing finger of the Palestinian peasant within the photographic frame is that the figure need not be physically present and observable in any specific image placed before the reader's eyes" (13). "Thus this image is there when it is not there" (14).

and the history of the Nuba, but also holding the northern man and the capital, Khartoum—symbol of northern Sudanese/"Arab" rule—accountable. To her, the northern man's mere presence was testimony for all of the north—in her memory, the perpetrators of the violence toward the Nuba Mountains. She was politicizing her memory of the violence, and her poetic pointing was a form of resistance. After she had left the building I mentioned to the man what she had said about northern Arabs dominating the Nuba. He said he had never been to the Nuba Mountains and had never met a Nuba woman. He did not consider himself a "northerner," nor an "Arab," but was from eastern Sudan, thus bringing in another perspective. Without invitation he added that the Nuba had helped the government all along, that they are collaborators, not victims.[4]

Pointing and shaming have also been powerful weapons in Darfur, another severe conflict area. We see the politics of memory in the "praise" songs of the "Arab" (Baggara) women Hakama singers, who tell the stories of battles in their own terms and are thought to make or break the reputations of male combatants (Cunnison 1966). Also, among the various ethnic groups of Darfur men are expected to be men, and women, women; and there is a great deal of shaming and pointing related to gender and sexuality. For example, one hears the charge from women: "You are not a man" (a woman trying to shame a man) or, a man or woman to a woman, "She is no man!" Again, women to women, "We need this peace so we can become women again."[5] These are all areas of resistance, building memories of the way the gender structure used to be before the conflict, including gestures toward how to shape gender relations in the future.

Women and women's bodies figure prominently in the Sudanese state's various attempts to reconfigure memory. The color of women and the color of men, within the context of the intricate "Arab" color

---

4 This comment is based on the fact that many Nuba men had been recruited into the army and had to fight against southerners and others, forever marking them in the eyes of some non-Nuba as collaborators.

5 Mariam Abdallah, Sudan Liberation Army rebel (Darfur rebel group), quoted by Opheera McDoom, Reuters journalist, whose blogs, tweets, and journalistic accounts are scattered throughout the internet. This quote is from a now-removed 2005 internet report (accessed July 1, 2004). For the Darfur ideology that women are women and men are men, see Willemse 2007.

code of the north, becomes a factor in Sudanese conflicts where men conquer partially through women, and lighter skin triumphs over darker skin, even if these differences are barely discernible to the eye of the outside observer. It is the *memory* of those colors, as they have been invented, that counts. A woman from Darfur reported that after a "devil on horseback" *(janjaweed)* raped her, he added, "Now you will have a whiter baby!"[6] She may have heard this, but she also just as easily may have constructed it to underscore the racialization of the Darfur struggle, one of the ways people explain the struggle to themselves and to each other. She, a brown-skinned woman, remembers a brown-skinned man making reference to his arguably lighter color after he raped her. She and her group have given the name "Arab" to these reputedly lighter-colored attackers, and that memory has been politicized as anti-Arab.

In Darfur, the government-supported militias, who are referred to popularly as the *janjaweed*, are reported by Amnesty International to have said to Darfurian women: "Slaves! Nubas! ... Your god is Omer al-Bashir" [president of Sudan]. "You blacks, you have spoilt the country! We are here to burn you. ... We will kill your husbands and sons and we will sleep with you! You will be our wives!" (Amnesty International 2004). The intersections of race, sex, gender, and violence have become ingrained in various survivors with whom I spoke. These links may well determine political relations for generations to come. How people process and act on these memories is political in and of itself.

Although racialized coding permeates Sudanese society in a number of ways, minoritized women have often resisted these racializations, as well as the state version of Islam and the general "official story." One northern Sudanese woman I interviewed, who described herself as a devout Muslim, said to me about the Islamist regime and the form of Islam being imposed on her after the Islamists came to power in 1989 that "I am not sure that these Islamic leaders remember our Islamic history all that well . . . I don't think they know what they are talking about."[7] She has had the fortitude, through her own memories and knowledge, to challenge the Islamist leaders' version of Islamic history.

---

6 Amnesty International 2004 (accessed October 12, 2011). See also Hale 2010: 105–113.

7 Name withheld upon request; interview by Hale, Omdurman, Sudan, July 16, 1988.

In 1988, just before the Islamists took power, I asked a forty-year-old, secondary school-educated Christian Arab from Khartoum what she thought of the Islamists coming to power. She exclaimed: "You cannot put a chain around the human being, because we have minds of our own. Unchained minds. Even if you chain my body, which is what some of these Islamic people would like to do, you cannot chain my mind."[8] These are defiant statements that challenge the authority and the epistemology of the Islamist state. I asked a Dinka woman from the former southern Sudan—a refugee in Cairo at the time—how she thought she might fit into a society designed by Islamists. She responded:

> *I was born a Dinka [in what is now South Sudan]. My father is a Dinka. I grew up near Juba [one of the major towns in South Sudan] where I went to school. War has torn us apart. Now we are only small fragments of what we used to be. I am not sure I can tell you what I am right now. . . . But I know I can tell you what I am not. I am not a Muslim. I am not one of them and I never will be.*[9]

I asked her if she felt excluded by Muslims. She responded, "You can only feel excluded by someone if you wanted to be one of them to start with!" I then followed up by asking how she sees *Christian* Arabs in the conflict, and she responded that "living with Muslims in the north has done something to them. They have forgotten how to be Christians or whatever they were before the Arabs ruined them."[10] Here she is suggesting that their memories of how to be Christians are not valid; otherwise they would not behave the way they do. She wants no part of it. She has constructed her own version of being Christian, or more accurately, of not being Muslim or Arab.

In an internet exchange, Fatima Ahmed Ibrahim, then the head of the Sudanese Women's Union, was expounding on what needed to be done to help the "backward" southerners. As a rebuttal, a southern Sudanese woman had this to say to the official story of the Sudanese Women's Union: "What has been said . . . can only remind us of the bitter history

---

8 Name withheld upon request; interview by Hale, Khartoum, July 22, 1988.
9 Name withheld upon request; interview by Hale, Cairo, August 18, 2003.
10 Name withheld upon request; interview by Hale, Cairo, August 19, 2003.

between the two parts of the country. We, Southern Sudanese women, cannot be objectified anymore and we can speak for ourselves."[11]

People are appropriating their own memories and their own histories. I witnessed first-hand many instances of the resistance by southern Sudanese women to northern women's overtures to be united with them as women, for example, at the United Nations Conference on Women in Beijing, 1995, and at a women's rights conference in Kampala, Uganda in 2003. The statements seem to say that southern and Nuba women have long memories of racism, religious persecution, and economic injustice. In 2003 in Kampala and in 2004 in Khartoum I witnessed southern and Nuba women telling northern-central women, almost like a threat, variations of "I remember; don't think that I have forgotten." These behaviors are similar to pointing, assigning blame, reminding the "perpetrator" that memories have been archived and will be politicized.

Most of the statements of resistance that I have heard were expressed by minoritized ethnic groups and were aimed at "Arabs." However, race, ethnicity, and class are not the only societal constructs where we can observe dissent and rebellions against the state and various group and official constructions of identity. I have been examining a number of case studies which demonstrate the different ways that men and women remember conflicts or the "heroic life" or the "everyday life of the Revolution," and the ways in which women's oftentimes idiosyncratic, accusing, ironic, and subversive retellings of their lives in conflict situations are forms of resistance. That this memory-work is oftentimes simultaneously spoken of and thought to be in alignment with what their male comrades have expounded is in harmony with much postcolonial theory, such as theories of ambivalence. I will be able to give only a few examples here.

Studies of Ambivalence

For many years I have been researching the narratives of members of the Sudanese Communist Party (SCP), especially the expressions of everyday life of the not-yet-lived revolution. I have been using some of the ideas from Srila Roy's study of the "heroic life" of the Naxalbari in Bengal (Roy

---

11 Cleto Rial et al. 1999, open letter addressed to the Sudanese community. Fatima Ahmed Ibrahim, at that point, had headed the Sudanese Women's Union for nearly 50 years. The SWU is an affiliate of the Sudanese Communist Party and is mainly associated with northern Sudanese/"Arabs."

2007). The "heroic life" is one that supposedly transcends the everyday and the ordinary. Yet, the "banal" vulnerabilities of everyday life continue to constitute the unseen, often unspoken. Women of the Naxalbari movement found life underground a site of vulnerability and powerlessness. I compare the Naxalbari case to Sudanese communists during the times when the Party was underground, when so much remained buried under a collective mythologizing of the "heroic life." Women and men of the SCP and its women's affiliate, the Sudanese Women's Union (SWU), remember and experience the "heroic life" very differently. Both may see themselves as living a revolution when in actuality the life of the Party and Union is mainly banal—the everyday of meetings and planning, of recruiting and indoctrinating. But the memory-work that is done in those activities creates a parallel and ambivalent world.

Men remember their male heroes—the union organizers, their executed secretary-general—and their life in prison, often saying these were the best years of their lives: being among men, telling stories, sharing everything, organizing for their return to freedom. Life in prison was seen not as the everyday, but as heroic activity.

In contrast, women of the families of these imprisoned "martyrs" tell of the sacrifices of keeping the family afloat financially when the men got arrested. Some silently resented that their husbands (in their view) did not try to avoid being arrested at moments of heightened political activity. Being arrested was, after all, a badge of honor for the men. I also heard resentments that the Party had so often interfered in their personal family lives, especially while the men were in prison. In contrast, men remember this as the Party taking care of wives of imprisoned martyrs. For many communist women married to communists, the domestic life they had to lead was another form of confinement, a banal life amid heroic ideas.

It is commonly said among leftist circles in Greater Khartoum that during times when the SCP was banned and driven underground, the men and the Party sometimes thrived. Above ground they got into internal conflicts. While the Party was underground there was solidarity; in prison they still had mobility to do political labor. However, while the Party was underground, the women lost their freedom of movement. They were not allowed to attend late-night meetings in "dubious neighborhoods" because their middle-classness would cause them to stand out and would expose everyone else—namely, the men. Therefore, when the SCP was underground, what resulted was another form of confinement for women.

There prevailed among women a kind of memory-work that was done in silence. Women kept quiet about sexual harassment and physical abuse, often remembering it as an inevitable sacrifice for the revolution, something to be endured as part of their role. Nothing that happened in private space—which was seen by men as outside the domain of the Party—should be used to discredit the Party. Furthermore, domestic violence was often seen as "something in the past" that "should be forgotten" so the Party could move on. Temporally, women remembered that sexual violence and physical abuse was a continuum; men saw these as "episodes," not a part of the everyday life of Party members. After all, the comrades were under stress and were not behaving in their "normal way," and should, therefore, not be held accountable for their trespasses.

Women keep quiet about any number of public, semi-public, and private acts of men of the Party, but their form of resistance is through memory-work—not only how they remember the events, but how they retell them in private and, perhaps, one day in public.

The expression of ambivalence has been a central feature of the hundreds of interviews I have carried out with Sudanese women over 54 years. The expressions of their memories of conflicts, crises, and violence are often coded, circumspect, and subversive, rarely straightforward. Besides, there is the problem that they are speaking to an outsider (me, the interviewer), someone toward whom they may also feel ambivalence. Nonetheless, difficult though it may be, the method of sifting through these memories, testimonies, and witnessing may lead us to very different perspectives on life in Sudan—both the banal and the heroic.

Toward the Archive and Repertoire: Some Ways of Remembering

Most commonly we think of archival memory as documents, literary texts, maps, letters, archaeological remnants, films, photographs, libraries, material collections, and so on. Although archives are thought of as material and in a fixed place, their value, relevance, or meaning may change over time. Repertoire, on the other hand, is thought of as something quite different. Performance theorist Diana Taylor defines repertoire as enacting "embodied memory" and includes performances, gestures, orality, movement, and dance. To her, "the repertoire requires presence: people participate in the production and reproduction of knowledge by 'being there,' being a part of the transmission."[12] In Taylor's interpretation, "embodied memory, because it is live, exceeds the archive's ability to capture it" (Taylor 2003:20). But this is not a binary between archive and repertoire. There is overlap and, according to Taylor, they usually work in tandem. One is more associated with the written word, a more hegemonic position (the "official story"); the other may be thought of as more subversive, anti-hegemonic, but that would be carrying the argument too far and falling into a binary. I have come to think of the memory-as-knowledge narratives, songs, and gossip that I have collected as more repertoire than archive.

The range of ways in which people, groups, and states try to remember the everyday and the extraordinary ("heroic") is myriad. People engage in memory maps; they photograph and map loss; they engage in autocartography, record in journals, collect memory books, keep scrapbooks, tell stories, write histories, give testimonies, bear witness, recite, gossip, sing songs, and point, among many other acts. Now that the internet is such a prominent feature in many people's lives, it is difficult even to fathom the endless mechanisms for remembering and transmitting, such as blogs and websites, that may be available to us in the future.

Sudanese women I have interviewed and lived with over the years tend not to keep journals, scrapbooks, or memory books, but write poetry instead, and some keep photo albums. Non-literate men might publicly recite their memories in poetic form. Women most commonly tell stories within private groups or family, or recite poetry or verses from the Quran, relating these verses to current grievances or conflicts. Perhaps it is only among the Hakama singers in Darfur (most commonly among the Baggara) that women publicly recite songs about the war exploits of the men—either praising or shaming them.[13] The purpose of these performances is to insist on some political participation, but the effect is to perform what they have remembered about a particular conflict and to

---

12 The ideas and quotes in this paragraph are from Taylor 2003:20.
13 See a much more ambivalent view of the Hakama singers who were accused of exhorting their men to rape Darfuri women and standing by, and then the shift by some to encouraging men toward peace: http://www.independent.co.uk/news/world/africa/can-songs-of-peace-bring-harmony-to-strifetorn-darfur-847479.html

remember it in their particular way, not as the men might have recalled it. These songs have become both archives and repertoires of memories of conflict, a contribution to our knowledge about war. However, the active social media involving women may soon change that a great deal, blurring the lines between archive and repertoire even further.

Concluding Remarks—What Do We Do with the Knowledge Retrieved from Memory-Work?

I have argued in this essay that for women in the contemporary conflict zones of various regions of Sudan, women's political and poetic memory-work can be a form of resistance. I have recounted some of the ways in which women and/or minoritized groups remember their work—as individuals or as a group—in resistance movements as a way of countering the "official story" of the state, the party, or the resistance movement itself. I have labeled this process "memory-work," but it is more than remembering. It is both a form of resisting and a form of knowledge production and retrieval.

My agenda in this essay has been to offer a glimpse of new methodological directions for analyzing nationalism, gender dynamics and the uses of women's bodies, localized or indigenous knowledge, memory, and the theorization of memory. I have attempted to politicize memory within the larger feminist agenda of struggle and resistance. Therefore, the contribution of my work is hopefully not just to state the obvious—that humans remember the same events and behaviors differently—but that they act on that difference and that this can be especially significant in conflict and/or post-conflict situations. The future of the various organizations and ethnic groups in struggle in Sudan, I predict, will be manifested in the gender dynamics that will emerge from the dissent that emanates from and is born of the politics of memory.

However, this still raises the question of what we do with the retrieval or recuperation of this form of knowledge, which often emanates from indigenous and localized forms. That is, how do we manage these forms of knowledge or facilitate local communities managing them? We can easily end up in our research project stating only that everyone has his/her own position or view of historical or local events and that all of these views are valid and authentic because they come out of lived experience. That is pretty extreme relativity. Setting up counterpoint sessions may be enlightening, that is, putting the "perpetrator" and the "victim" side by side in the telling of the story. However, we might still end up with a he said/she said situation. Setting up focus groups might be a way for people to examine their perceptions in relation to others' perceptions and to weigh these accordingly.

Those of us who work with qualitative methods are often challenged to demonstrate that our findings are as valid as the findings of those doing quantitative studies. We are, therefore, compelled to ask whether all knowledge is equally valid and of equal value. In my work on the politics of memory, there remains the vexing question of whether or not some memories are more valuable than others. Nonetheless, if we engage in counterpoints to our memories and check and counter-check the testimonies, the chances are higher for retrieving valuable information and being able to manage it, because of the ways in which we have retrieved it and because of the position of the interlocutor from whom we gained the knowledge. Working with these methods within conflict zones may yield partial resolutions, which may be all we can ask for, for now. These are still mediated memories and our methodologies for working out the blurred lines between archives and repertoires are limited.

References

Amnesty International. 2004. "Sudan: Darfur: Rape as a Weapon of War: Sexual Violence and Its Consequences." http://www.amnesty-usa.org/node/55614

Cleto Rial, Sarah, et al. 1999. "Shall We Keep Quiet . . . or Ignore? In Response to an Article by Ustaza Fatima Ahmed Ibrahim." Sudanese@list.msu.edu.

Cunnison, Ian. 1966. *Barrara Arabs: Power and the Lineage in a Sudanese Nomad Tribe.* Oxford: Oxford University Press.

Hale, Sondra. 2010. "Rape as Marker and Erasure of Difference: Darfur and the Nuba Mountains (Sudan)." In Laura Sjoberg and Sandra Kia, eds. *Gender, War, and Militarism*, 105–113. Santa Barbara: Praeger, ABC-CLIO.

Hodgekin, Katharine, and Susannah Radstone. 2003. *Contested Pasts: The Politics of Memory.* New York: Routledge.

Roy, Srila. 2007. "The Everyday Life of the Revolution," *South Asia Research*, 27(2): 187–204.

Slyomovics, Susan. 1998. *The Object of Memory: Arab and Jew Narrate the Palestinian Village.* Philadelphia: University of Pennsylvania Press.
Taylor, Diana. 2003. *The Archive and the Repertoire: Performing Cultural Memory in the Americas.* Durham, NC: Duke University Press.
Willemse, Karin. 2007. *One Foot in Heaven: Narratives on Gender and Islam in Darfur.* Leiden: Brill.

CHAPTER 3

Women's Activism and Contending Narratives of Liberation in South Africa

Noor Nieftagodien

South African historiography has experienced a major transformation since the early 1990s, accompanied by an emphasis on and proliferation of histories of the anti-apartheid struggle, which were prompted by two principal imperatives: to redress the racial imbalance in the histories produced under apartheid and to celebrate the histories of liberation movements. These crucial exercises of historical rewriting occurred in the political context of the transition to democracy and accession to power by the African National Congress (ANC), while drawing intellectual inspiration from social history and the "people's history" movement in the 1980s. As a result, uncovering and recording the histories of the black experience became a necessary and important focus of new historical knowledge production. History curricula at schools and universities and published material circulating in the public domain are now fundamentally different from what existed 25 years ago. In this process, new master narratives have been produced, especially in relation to liberation histories. While gesturing appropriately to the counter-hegemonic traditions that shaped the production of people's histories during the liberation struggle, these narratives have, however, become tied to new political imperatives such as nation-building, reconciliation, and affirming the ANC's hegemony. Nelson Mandela's autobiography, *Long Walk to Freedom*, in many respects created a template for liberation histories, especially biographies, which are overwhelmingly ANC-centric and teleological. Furthermore, these struggle narratives tend to venerate an ideal figure of the heroic freedom fighter: an armed black man.

Consequently, and despite routine disclaimers, women continue to be marginalized and excluded from the struggle narratives. Where the role of women is acknowledged, they are invariably inserted into pre-existing master narratives and follow conventional and problematic gendered tropes: as 'mothers of the nation' and supporters and helpers. In other words, as South African feminist scholars have argued, women usually appear as ancillaries in the struggle led by men. This chapter, first and foremost, makes the rather obvious critique of the view that women were secondary actors in the struggle for emancipation. Such a position is empirically unsustainable because black women were central actors throughout the liberation struggle and, at particular moments, critical in shaping the character of the resistance movements. Drawing on oral histories of women and reading existing archives differently, the chapter briefly discusses key moments of women's resistance, especially in the 1940s and 1950s. Specifically, attention is paid to popular insurgent movements that could be interpreted as formative in struggles by Africans to make claims to rights to the city during this period when the liberation movements were fundamentally reconfigured. However, while it is crucial to insert women into existing narratives of struggle, such an exercise is insufficient and problematic. Following feminist scholarship, it is equally important to employ different analytical frameworks in order better to comprehend the varied nature of women's struggles.

In fact, feminist scholars have mounted various critiques of the master narratives of the liberation struggle. Thozama April has challenged the way in which a leading woman intellectual of the early twentieth century, Charlotte Maxeke, was appropriated by the ANC. Her life story was reconfigured to become synonymous with the party's history despite the fact that her interests and activism extended far beyond the ANC. These struggle histories cast the role of women in "predetermined terms as an effect of the generosity of male figures" and in the case of Maxeke transformed her "into the symbolic mother of the nation" after her death (April 2012:97, 106). Furthermore, the celebration of the male-led nationalist movement tends to neglect Maxeke, among others, as an intellectual and feminist. According to April, "the nationalist narratives of the struggle do not engage in a meaningful dialogue with Maxeke's ideas about, for instance, gender inequality, 'native womanhood,' justice, education, health and employment" (April 2012:97, 106). She therefore argues for histories that critically engage the varied and complex role of women's resistance by simultaneously challenging male-centric historical narratives and the continuation of male-dominated politics.

Feminist scholars have for some time been critical of the problematic new narratives of liberation histories written from the mid-1990s, which often seem oblivious of feminist and social history literature that began to make an impression on scholarship in the 1980s. Notwithstanding ritual acknowledgments of the role of women, the new scholarship usually reverts to conventional and outdated modes of inserting women in struggle histories. Healy-Clancy has thus bemoaned the persistent focus on formal political organizations, which "valorises women's presence in the spaces where they were in fact least common—the halls of the male-led ANC" (Healy-Clancy 2012:455). In this approach, she argues, "prominent women make appearances as colleagues and kin" of powerful men. Largely absent in these studies are women's groups, the family, and various non-institutional structures that were far more central to women's politics than the political parties were.

Despite the paucity of references on the politics of black women in official archives, Hassim, Walker, and other feminist scholars have uncovered rich histories of individuals, women's social groups, episodes of struggle (at local and national levels), and a range of political activities, all of which contributed to the complex constitution of "the struggle."[1] These accounts and analyses were in part a response to the relative absence of women in dominant narratives of the struggle. Walker explains that the histories of formal organizations, invariably led by men, predominated because the voices of women, especially of black women, were largely missing. "Women simply disappear from our view of the past," she suggests, because of their marginalization in official records (Walker 1990:2–3). However, this body of scholarship did far more than simply insert women into existing narratives; in fact, it mounted a strident critique of the representations of women's struggles in the existing literature, which tended to confine women to specific roles in the predominant political organizations. For Hassim, women were represented as auxiliaries: "For most of the twentieth century, women were second-class members of the ANC" and "the role of the Women's Section from the time the ANC went into exile in

---

1 For example, Hassim 2004; Walker 1990; Bradford 1987; Wells 1993.

the 1960s had been primarily to act as the movement's social worker" (Hassim 2004:434–435). By focusing their attention on women's struggles, these two scholars have demonstrated both the importance of the role of women in the main liberation movements that transcend predetermined gendered roles and highlighted the autonomy of their own struggles. Helen Bradford's study of beer protests undertaken by women in the 1920s extends this argument by pointing out that the dominant literature relegated "female beer protests ... to the sphere of the 'backward-looking' resistance by conservative, non-feminist women defending 'traditional' rights." It is an approach characterized by the denial of the "feminist impulses" in these struggles, reflecting a failure to focus attention on predominantly female spheres, such as the family and home, which are sites of "women's most intimate insubordination." In order properly to comprehend women's struggles, analysts need to transcend the conventional analytical straitjackets of nationalism and class, and acknowledge the importance of patriarchy (Bradford 1987:293). Bradford and Walker insist that the personal sphere (including the family) is profoundly political, and the struggles in these spaces are constitutive of broader resistance politics. Whereas men invariably dominated formal or public political spaces (the main political parties and public meetings), women tended to be more influential in the constitution of protest politics in what may be described as informal spaces, in locations such as yards, streets, and associational networks. This chapter considers these issues by focusing attention on an iconic event in the history of the anti-apartheid struggle: the Women's March of 1956.

Women's March of 1956

Few moments exemplify the importance of women's struggle better than the historic march of August 9, 1956 when approximately 20,000 women marched to the Union Buildings in Pretoria, the seat of white power, to hand over a petition to the prime minister demanding the abolition of the extension of passes to African women. Until then only African men were forced to carry passes, which placed severe restrictions on their mobility. From the early 1950s the apartheid government sought to bring women under similar state surveillance in response to the rapid urbanization of African women and their involvement in various forms of political resistance and what the state deemed anti-social activities. Led by the Federation of South African Women (FED-SAW), the march was the culmination of months of organization by women activists across the country to collect signatures and generally to mobilize opposition to the state's restrictions against African women. Since then, the historic march of 1956 has become etched in collective memory and history as a singularly important moment of women's resistance. After 1994, it was officially memorialized with the declaration of August 9 as National Women's Day. In so doing, the African National Congress (ANC) government has appropriately acknowledged the role of women in the history of struggle against apartheid.

However, a closer scrutiny of the ways in which this history has been produced reveals serious problems. In broad terms, the 1956 march has been subsumed under a dominant narrative of the liberation struggle that has emphasized the central role of the ANC and its male leaders. According to this narrative, the radicalization of the ANC was inaugurated with the founding of the ANC Youth League (led by key male intellectuals), which orchestrated a leadership coup in the late 1940s that led to the launch of mass struggles in the 1950s: these included the defiance campaign, the anti-Bantu Education struggles, resistance against forced removals, the adoption of the Freedom Charter, the women's march, and the anti-pass campaign. On the one hand, this version of history correctly places the women's struggles in the broad anti-apartheid movement. On the other hand, it underplays and even ignores the autonomous struggles by women in the years preceding the march, which shaped the character of the latter and account for its success.

In fact, there has been a constant tension between the national liberation movements and women's struggle for emancipation. When it was founded in 1954, FEDSAW adopted the Women's Charter, which, according to Hassim, was "firmly located within the anti-apartheid struggle, [but] also sought to address the specifics of women's oppression" (Hassim 2014:33). As such, the new movement asserted an independent role for women in the broader national liberation struggle and went about campaigning and organizing on women's own terms, which often created problems between male leaders and women activists. Following the march on the Union Buildings, women continued to campaign against passes in localities across the country, resulting in the arrests of thousands. During the course of these struggles, FEDSAW found male leaders opposed to their decision to defy the authorities and remain in jail. Although women were in the forefront of the anti-pass struggles between 1956 and 1958, when new anti-pass campaigns were launched in 1959–60 they were effectively sidelined. For example, the ANC's symbolic pass-burning activities were almost exclusively undertaken by its male leaders. The Pan Africanist Congress (PAC), the allegedly more radical breakaway from the ANC, was even more deliberate in its efforts to marginalize women in its anti-pass campaign. The pamphlet issued by the organization to mobilize for the fateful anti-pass march in Sharpeville in March 1960 called on women to stay at home to perform their domestic duties, while men went about executing the struggle. As it turned out, women ignored the attempt to exclude them from a struggle in which they were primary actors, and many were killed when police opened fire at the demonstrators. What the 1956 march and the anti-pass campaign of this period highlighted was that women were not mere ancillaries in a male-led struggle but were prominent in the national liberation movement. Passes were integral to the state's technologies of surveillance and oppression of African people, and thus were identified by the liberation movements as one of the critical targets of attack in the struggle against apartheid. The state's decision to extend passes to women in the 1950s was part of a suite of interventions designed specifically to bring African women, who were perceived as being predisposed to radicalism, under control. It was implemented in response to the proliferation of location-based popular protests in the 1940s in which women increasingly asserted collective and leading roles. The anti-pass mobilization of the mid 1950s drew on these traditions of women's autonomous mobilization in urban working-class communities.

Women in Protest Movements

Unprecedented industrialization and urbanization in South Africa beginning in the 1930s, and especially in the 1940s, created the conditions for an upsurge in popular struggles. Based mainly in the black locations and squatter settlements, these struggles were usually centered on subsistence issues. Between the mid 1930s and mid 1940s the urban African population registered a sharp increase, from about 1.1 million to nearly 1.8 million people. Crucially, for the first time the number of Africans outnumbered whites in urban centers, thereby signaling a qualitative shift in the character of the country's towns and cities. Of equal significance was the fact that the number of Africans living in urban areas nearly doubled, from about 350,000 to 650,000, over the same period (Fine and Davis 1991:14, 156). The sharp increase in the black urban population was not met with corresponding provision of basic services, resulting in high levels of overcrowding and a general deterioration of living conditions in black locations. There was an explosion in the number of tenants and sub-tenants, as every available space in houses and yards was filled to capacity. But even this proved inadequate and, inevitably, there was a proliferation of squatter settlements. At the end of the Second World War there were approximately 100,000 squatters around Johannesburg alone.

Single women were disproportionately affected by the lack of housing because municipal houses catered only for married couples and families, and were registered in the names of men. Women therefore constituted a high proportion of squatters and sub-tenants, placing them in the forefront of campaigns against evictions and for housing. The position of African women in urban areas was further compromised by their limited access to formal employment, forcing them into survivalist livelihood strategies in the precarious informal sector, such as illegal beer brewing. These factors contributed to women featuring prominently in local protest movements over housing, rent and bus fare increases, and state surveillance. They represented a powerful assertion by the black working class of the right to be present in urban areas and to claim corresponding rights in the city, especially a decent living and access to affordable public services. In the course of these struggles, new movements were created, usually independent of the existing formal political parties and usually focused on specific socioeconomic issues in particular localities, as well as being characterized by significant participation and even leadership of women.

An early example of these movements occurred in response to the state's implementation of lodgers' fees in the early 1930s as a new revenue stream in black locations. This new cost placed enormous strain on the standard of living of poor black communities, who were already adversely affected by the Great Depression: income levels declined, inflation increased, and poverty levels soared. Therefore, when the municipal authorities of Germiston, an industrial town east of Johannesburg, decided to impose a two-shilling lodgers' fee on the residents of Dukathole, the black location attached to the town, there was an outcry and the existing organizations immediately embarked on a campaign to oppose the measure. However, women of the location quickly expressed their disappointment with the ineffectual campaign led by men and created the Women's League of Justice (WLJ) to launch a more militant struggle. Initiated by Sofia Koerkop and other members of the local Wives' Association, the new movement grew rapidly and within months claimed a membership of between 1,000 and 2,000, easily eclipsing the formal political organizations. The WLJ drew support from the existing, relatively small women's associations, often linked to churches, as well as from the more pervasive informal networks of women living as sub-tenants and in the overcrowded yards. At its height, the movement played the leading role in challenging the authority of the local administration and in June 1933 led a march of nearly 1,000 women to the town council (Bonner and Nieftagodien 2012:47). What the protests in this location revealed was the role of independent protest movements and women in particular in challenging policies of the state. These events were also a harbinger of an explosion of protests across the country in the 1940s.

Described as arguably the most significant instance of African resistance during the Second World War, the Alexandra bus boycott witnessed thousands of residents of the freehold location walking about 12 kilometers to and from Johannesburg every day. For Nelson Mandela, who was living in Alexandra at the time, the sight of thousands of township residents protesting daily confirmed the emerging political power of the urban black working class and marked the moment when he was transformed from an 'observer' to a 'participant' in the struggle for black emancipation (Mandela 1995:100). The historic boycott was led by the Emergency Transport Action Committee (ETAC), comprising prominent local activists from various political groups. One of the outstanding figures in this movement was Lillian Tshabalala, who was already heavily involved in a network of independent socialists and local members of the Communist Party of South Africa (CPSA). In September 1943, these political groups launched the African Democratic

Party (ADP) in response to the perceived lethargy of the established political parties, particularly the ANC, in the context of mounting popular struggles (Bonner and Nieftagodien 2008:71).

Tshabalala's activism and intellectual contribution to women's politics preceded her involvement in Alexandra's bus boycotts. She cut her intellectual and political teeth while studying in the US between 1912 and 1930, where she was also employed as a teacher and was involved in supporting welfare programs among the African-American community in Connecticut. When she returned home, Tshabalala immediately immersed herself in women's activism, becoming a founding member of the Daughters of Africa, a movement that established a network of women activists across the country to highlight and campaign on issues affecting women (Healy-Clancy 2012). According to Healy-Clancy, Tshabalala's political and intellectual talents were crucial to the success of the Daughters of Africa (2012:469).

Therefore, by the time she settled in Alexandra in 1940, Tshabalala was already a leader of an established organization that operated autonomously from the formal male-controlled political movements. She set about launching a local chapter of the Daughters of Africa in the township, which brought her into contact with Josie Mpama (Healy-Clancy 2012:465–470), a key figure in the Communist Party of South Africa and one of the leaders of the successful struggle against lodgers' fees in the town of Potchefstroom in 1929–30 (Edgar 2005:5–13). Mpama was formidable. She not only stood up against the conservative white local administration, but in the course of the struggle she recruited the majority of the black location's residents to the party. Thereafter, she continued to be involved in working-class struggles and active in the internal disputes of the Communist Party, placing her on a different ideological trajectory from Lillian Tshabalala, who was involved in anti-Stalinist and independent socialist organizations.

Tshabalala's activism was not confined to explicitly left-wing party politics. She was also a prominent member of the African Women's Brigade, which the contemporary activist Miriam Basner described as consisting of "formidable churchwomen and beer brewers who made themselves responsible for the township's solidarity and good order—especially among the faint-hearted or riotously disposed men" (Hirson 1990:139, 144).

It is important to note that women participated in the bus boycott not only as individual supporters but also through their own organizations, which were among the most effective constituencies in terms of engendering unity and solidarity. The success of the bus boycott ultimately depended on the willingness of residents to undertake the long daily march, the mobilization for which largely occurred in the streets and yards of the township, where women played a central role.

A major source of contention between the authorities and African women was the former's determination to root out domestic beer brewing. For large numbers of women, who were effectively excluded from the labor market, illicit beer brewing was the only source of income that allowed them not only to survive but also to be relatively autonomous from men. The state sought to establish a monopoly over the production and sale of beer to control the consumption of liquor by African men, and, critically, to protect a vital source of revenue. From the late 1920s, thousands of women across the country, but especially in the rapidly expanding urban locations, were daily involved in confrontations with the police, engendering innumerable points of resistance, albeit typically individual and ephemeral. However, on occasion the state's policies with regard to beer brewing produced collective resistance. A case in point was the struggle in Payneville, the black location of the mining town of Springs, located about 50 kilometers east of Johannesburg. Here the struggle over control of beer brewing dominated local political struggles for most of the 1940s. The municipality's decision to erect a beer hall in order to monopolize this lucrative source of income, coupled with an intensification of raids against domestic brewers, caused an escalation in tensions between the state and women. Initially these struggles were spearheaded by the African Protection League, whose leader was the indefatigable Dinah Maile. Her rise to prominence in struggles throughout the 1940s brought her into the orbit of left-wing politics and eventually into the ranks of the CPSA (Hirson 1990:84–86).

The key struggle in this protracted dispute occurred in 1945 when the women of the location organized a boycott of the beer hall. On July 8 of that year, the CPSA called a public meeting where Maile's defiant speech and support for domestic brewing were enthusiastically endorsed.[2]

---

2 CAD, Department of Native Affairs Files (NTS) 7676, 110/322, Report of the Springs Police District Commandant, 1945.

Thereafter, women began to actively mobilize: demonstrations, marches, and meetings took place regularly as the pressure to close the beer hall mounted,[3] culminating on July 22 in a demonstration by 2,000 women at the beer hall to prevent men from entering. Unsurprisingly, the police violently dispersed the demonstrators, triggering a riot that rapidly spread through the location.[4] The main demand of the protestors—the closure of the beer hall—was not accepted by the authorities, who were determined not to make concessions to "riotous women." Protests continued throughout the 1940s, albeit on a smaller scale, but in 1949 the struggles once again escalated when the Residents Protest Committee was formed to campaign against the "indirect method of taxation" represented by the beer hall.[5] At the same time the authorities were also unable to stop domestic brewing, reflecting the determination of women to continue their defiance of the authorities. The struggle in Payneville highlighted quite dramatically that women had to wage a struggle on two fronts: against the white municipal authorities and against the men of the location, many of whom deliberately undermined the call for a boycott of the beer hall. Helen Bradford's compelling account of African women's protests in 1929 against beer halls and for the legalization of domestic beer brewing in several towns in Natal's countryside resonates powerfully with the protests in Payneville and other locations (Bradford 1987). Her narrative challenges the view that militant confrontation with white authority was the exclusive domain of radical men (especially youth) and that women at best performed auxiliary roles in this contestation. In so doing, it potentially unsettles what Kros (following Unterhalter) has described as "the overbearing narrative of 'heroic masculinity'" (Kros 2012:253; Unterhalter 2000).

Dominant narratives of the radicalization of black politics in the 1940s emphasize the role of men in general and of ANC Youth League leaders in particular. Their contributions are regarded as more important because of their direct effect on the leadership and program of

---

3   CAD, NTS 7676, 110/322, Report of the Springs Police District Commandant, 1945.
4   CAD, NTS 7676, 110/322, Report of the Non-European Affairs Manager on the Disturbances in Payneville, July 22, 1945.
5   CAD, MSP 1/3/5/1/28, Minutes of the Public Health and Non-European Affairs Committee, "Protest against the Proposal to Use Profits from the Sale of Kaffir Beer for Housing Funds," 1949.

the ANC. In this rendition of struggle history the myriad struggles by women, which were crucial in transforming black locations into contentious spaces that, in turn, created the conditions for the mass struggles of the 1950s, are often marginalized. Furthermore, these struggles, and the movements and leaders which they produced, laid the foundations on which the anti-pass struggles of the 1950s were built. Without these locally based movements, the campaigning and collection of tens of thousands of signatures may not have succeeded.

If the role of women in popular protest movements has been downplayed, then their participation in the underground movements of the 1960s has been even more neglected. Underground activities are associated with danger and sacrifice, akin to armed confrontation, and are thus perceived as quintessentially male spaces. In reality, women were arguably even more pivotal in maintaining the fragmented underground presence of the liberation movements in conditions of severe repression.

The Underground
Following the Sharpeville massacre in 1960, the state banned the main black political organizations and unleashed a wave of severe repression, resulting in the promulgation of a battery of draconian laws, mass detentions, extrajudicial killings, and widespread intimidation of activists. In response, the ANC and the Pan Africanist Congress (PAC) decided in 1961 to embark on armed struggle and to reorganize themselves in exile. Two broad consequences followed from these circumstances: first, the armed struggle became the centerpiece of the political strategy of the liberation organization; second, the internal movement, comprising disparate networks of activists, was forced into clandestine mode. Histories of the armed struggle have generally been framed in heroic terms, with the military-clad and armed male soldier as the iconic freedom fighter. The fact that Nelson Mandela was the first commander-in-chief of the ANC's military wing (Umkhonto we Sizwe—'spear of the nation') reinforced the idea that armed men were responsible for South Africa's liberation. In so doing, the role of the internal underground, consisting mostly of people not directly involved in the liberation armies, has tended to be marginalized. This is especially significant because women activists were absolutely critical in keeping the underground alive. They operated under incredibly difficult and dangerous conditions, and had

to deal with despondency and fear among large swathes of the black population, including activists. Yet they managed to keep the idea of the liberation struggle alive, and from the late 1960s began to constitute an important link between the nascent black student movement and the older generation of activists.

Albertina Sisulu, Winnie Mandela, Helen Joseph, Mary Moodley, and Liz Abrahams were among the best-known of these women activists who, despite personal hardships (including banning orders and stints in detention), persisted with their political work throughout the dark days of the 1960s. There were many other less well-known women activists who played equally crucial roles in the underground during this period. The women of the Naidoo family were one such group whose contribution to the underground work had largely been forgotten but which has recently been retrieved through oral histories. The family has a long tradition of political activism in South Africa, starting with the prominent role of Thambi Naidoo, who worked with Gandhi in passive resistance campaigns in the early twentieth century. Decades later, his son Roy Naidoo became a leader of the Transvaal Indian Congress in the ANC's mass campaigns in the 1950s. His son, Indres, was among the first to be arrested for belonging to the ANC's military wing and was sentenced to ten years in prison. The histories of these male members of the family are firmly entrenched in the narratives of the ANC and its Congress partners. Much less is known about the contributions by the women, including Roy's spouse, Ama Naidoo. She was an activist in her own right, while raising a family, and suffered harassment and detention. Already in the 1950s her home in the working-class suburb of Doornfontein (Johannesburg) was an important hub of political activity. In the 1960s it became a vital node in the informal and clandestine networks of activism. It was a meeting point for clergy, unionists, students, and older activists. One of Ama's daughters, Shanti, worked for progressive legal organizations while being associated with underground networks.[6] Shanti was arrested in 1969 and held in solitary confinement for a year for refusing to give evidence in the trial of Winnie Mandela, who was a key figure in an underground structure based in Soweto.

In the late 1960s, a new generation of young activists began to link up with older activists in parts of Soweto and Johannesburg, with the aim

---
6 Interview, Shanti Naidoo.

of re-establishing some semblance of a political presence in the township. Winnie Mandela, Rita Ndzinga, and Joyce Sikhakhane, together with senior male trade unionists, were the main people involved in this endeavor. Between 1966 and 1969 this group worked with groups of youth to provide them with basic political education. Snuki Zikalala, who was a leader of the youth involved in this underground network, recalled that "Joyce [Sikhakhane] gave us ANC politics. Then in the second week we organized another meeting at my place. What she did, she brought Samson Ndou [then] Ndzinga [who] started giving us Marxist literature and ANC literature and then we started reading about the struggle itself" (Nieftagodien and Gaule 2012:61). After months of political education, a more formal structure, with cells consisting of between five and ten people each, was created. At its height in 1969 there were an estimated 300 people involved, making it one of the most extensive underground structures in the country at the time. All manner of guises were utilized to activate this network, which typically involved women organizing extracurricular classes for students and tea parties at their homes. Their plans were not elaborate and concentrated on two principal matters: educating a new generation of activists and maintaining a clandestine network that would later become involved in the rebuilding of the internal liberation movement and provide more active support for the exile organizations.

Conclusion

It is evident that women were protagonists in the struggle against apartheid, both in the principal liberation parties and in the popular protest movements. They were generally more prominent and active in the latter, the building blocks for which were the contentious location spaces in which women forged autonomous politics. Protest movements of the 1940s contributed in important ways to the creation of a generation of women activists who became involved in more formal organizations in the 1950s and were prominent in the wave of anti-apartheid struggles in that decade, including the anti-pass march of 1956. The growing body of historical research on anti-apartheid struggle has relied very heavily on the collection of oral testimonies, with an emerging focus on life histories of women. Attention is also being given to non-party resistance, which has led to an excavation of activism in spaces where women have been more involved. By analyzing resistance politics from the vantage point of the experiences of women activists, different insights and narratives are being produced. Thus it is possible that a new wave of historical rewriting may be inaugurated, hopefully anchored in radical feminist scholarship.

References

April, Thozama. 2012. "Charlotte Maxeke: A Celebrated and Neglected Figure in History." In O. Badsha, N. Erlank, A. Lissoni, N. Nieftagodien, and J. Soske, eds. *One Hundred Years of the ANC*, 97–107. Johannesburg: Wits University Press.

Bonner, P.L., and N. Nieftagodien. 2008. *Alexandra—A History*. Johannesburg: Wits University Press.

———. 2012. *Ekurhuleni: The Making of an Urban Region*. Johannesburg: Wits University Press.

Bradford, H. 1987. "'We Are Now the Men': Women's Beer Protests in the Natal Countryside, 1929." In B. Bozzoli, ed. *Class, Community and Conflict: South African Perspectives*, 292–323. Johannesburg: Ravan Press.

Edgar, R. 2005. *The Making of an African Communist: Edwin Thabo Mofutsanyana and the Communist Party of South Africa, 1927–1939*. Pretoria: Unisa Press.

Fine, R., and D. Davis. 1991. *Beyond Apartheid: Labour and Liberation in South Africa*. Johannesburg: Ravan Press.

Hassim, S. 2004. "Nationalism, Feminism and Autonomy: The ANC in Exile and the Question of Women," *Journal of Southern African Studies*, 30(3): 433–455.

———. 2014. *The ANC Women's League*. Johannesburg: Jacana Publishers.

Healy-Clancy, M. 2012. "Women and the Problem of the Family in Early African Nationalist History and Historiography," *South African Historical Journal*, 64(3): 450–471.

Hirson, B. 1990. *Yours for the Union: Class and Community Struggles in South Africa*. Johannesburg: Wits University Press.

Kros, C. 2012. "Lives in the Making: The Possibilities and Impossibilities of Autobiography with Reference to the Case of Amina Cachalia," *South African Historical Journal*, 64(2): 236–255.

Mandela, N. 1995. *Long Walk to Freedom*. London: Abacus.
Nieftagodien, N., and S. Gaule. 2012. *Orlando West: A Photographic History*. Johannesburg: Wits University Press.
Unterhalter, E. 2000. "The Work of the Nation: Heroic Masculinity in South African Autobiographical Writing of the Anti-Apartheid Struggle," *European Journal of Development Research*, 12(2): 157–178.
Walker, C. 1982. *Women and Resistance in South Africa*. Cape Town: David Philip.
———. 1990. "Women and Gender in Southern Africa to 1945: An Overview." In C. Walker, ed. *Women and Gender in Southern Africa to 1945*, 1–32. Cape Town: David Philip.
Wells, J. 1993. *We Now Demand! The History of Women's Resistance to Pass Laws in South Africa*. Johannesburg: Wits University Press, 1993.

CHAPTER 4

The Production of Alternative Knowledge: Political Participation of Palestinian Women since the 1930s: A Case Study

Faiha Abdulhadi

Introduction

While mainstream history is written by the victorious (Sayegh 1980), social history is the story of ordinary people who make history. It is the history of marginalized women and men. When history is written from a popular and democratic perspective, it documents the experiences of ordinary people overlooked by more formal history, and involves people in formulating their own history, highlighting the voices of the voiceless. In this way, another narrative emerges alongside the official one, in agreement with the recorded narrative at times, and disagreeing with it at other times. As it adds its stories, the narrative contributes to the production of an alternative knowledge of reality, the events, and the men and women who created those events.

This study aims to rewrite history from a perspective that recognizes the effective contribution of women, and document the experiences of women, who played a major part in history making, but did not participate in the act of writing history. Narrating women's experiences leads to an interaction with and a challenge of the dominant discourses on female vulnerability, stereotyping, and subordination, and contributes to the production of an alternative discourse, which makes women visible and gives them a voice.

A feminist oral history makes space for women to express their views and to touch base with their feelings and emotions. This is accomplished through an interview that is attentive, participatory, and characterized by empathic listening. A feminist approach to oral history is grounded in a deep understanding of women. It approaches women through women, to listen consciously to their voices and make them heard. As a multidisciplinary perspective, it makes use of a wide range of disciplines, revealing the artificiality of the separation between academic disciplines, which prevents a deep knowledge of women (Tonkin 1995). This research approach provides freedom and flexibility for both the female researchers and the female narrators, rendering a deeper knowledge of the psychological nature of women (Gluck and Patai 1991) and deconstructing the dominant values, which fail to recognize the experiences of women as a major component in history making. Thus a new set of values can be formed, allowing the integration and the harmonization of the experiences of women and men (Elsadda 1999:168).

In this study, an attempt is made to listen to the two contradicting voices of women: the public voice, which they have practiced for so long, and the hidden voice, which they have long learned to suppress.

What women reveal about themselves does not reflect an objective description of their lives, but tends to originate from a cultural background, and a cultural content that has a historical authority which limits and restricts the activities of women. Accordingly, the uncovering of the language and meaning that women utilize in their daily lives helps us become aware of the social forces and ideas that have an impact on them. (Anderson, Armitage, Jack, and Wittner 1987:103)

A feminist perspective pays attention to body language and the related emotional reactions, to the movements of the hands, the feet, and the face as a whole, as well as the details of the eyebrows, the lips, the eyes, and the mouth. It asks the women about the meanings of the expressions they use, especially the ones they use to describe themselves.

The Political Contribution of Palestinian Women in the 1930s

This chapter introduces some of the research findings of a project to document the role of Palestinian women since the 1930s (Abdulhadi 2006a). The aim is to make women visible and to shed light on the history of women's struggle for the benefit of future generations of Palestinian and Arab young men and women, and to enable women to actively participate in rebuilding the Palestinian archives and reproduce knowledge. Over the course of the project, the prominent status of Palestinian women, from the 1930s to the mid 1960s, became evident—a status that is deeply entrenched in popular Palestinian memory. Furthermore, the research included the names of many women overlooked by written history, despite their presence in the memory of many of their contemporaries.

Previous research studies on the political participation of women during the period from the 1930s until the mid 1960s were found to be missing. Therefore this period was selected as well as the areas where the research was to be conducted and the gender of the narrators. The vast majority of the 155 narrators who were interviewed were women: this unequal ratio of men to women served the purpose of the project as we were able to record the political participation of women in the 1930s while recognizing the need to record the narrations of some men who were their contemporaries.

In our research we relied on populated areas, taking into consideration the distribution of narrators in each area in accordance with two age groups: over 75 years old and over 55 years old. In addition we took into account the division of women into urban, rural, educated, and illiterate groups.

The study attempted to cover the areas of the Palestinian presence both inside and outside Palestine: West Bank, Gaza Strip, the 1948 areas, and Jerusalem in Palestine, in addition to Jordan, Syria, Lebanon, and Egypt. Seventeen women researchers participated in the research project.

In order to probe into some of the blind spots in mainstream history regarding women's political participation, the following questions were asked: Did women participate in politics during that period? If yes, was the participation of women fundamental? What was the role of rural women in politics during that period? Responses to the questions confirmed the participation of Palestinian women in political life in the 1930s, and their contribution was essential, not marginal or unsubstantial as many mainstream historians claim (al-Shihabi 1994).

Mainstream history (Mughanam 1986) has acknowledged the participation of urban women, highlighting their great courage in standing up against the British occupation forces, as they submitted petitions and wrote articles in local newspapers. It also documents their participation through the Palestinian Women's Union, founded in 1921; in the Palestinian political conferences, where women's political conferences were held; and their contribution to the Arab women's conferences held in support of the Palestinian cause: for instance, they formed a large delegation to participate in the conference held by Huda Sha'rawi in Egypt in 1938. Rural women, however, were not adequately recognized. They played a different role from urban women, as they participated effectively in all forms of armed struggle. However, history recognizes only one aspect of their participation: providing the revolutionaries with food and water, and transporting weapons and ammunition to them. Previous oral history narratives have not succeeded in altering the recurring stereotype of the role of rural women in the 1930s, reduced to providing supplies for the revolutionaries, transporting weapons, and inciting the men going to battle. This is partly due to dominant cultural values that encouraged women to understate their achievements.

The initial responses of women narrators to questions about their roles differed significantly from their responses after an amicable bond had been established with the interviewer.

Interviewer: *What did women do when you were a kid?*

The narrators gave quick and similar responses:

Absolutely nothing: they milk, churn, lie on the rugs in the fields, that's what we Arabs do, we're all farmers.[1]

Our work is preparing food, drinks, meals, and feasts; it all revolves around housework.[2]

---

1 Interview with Khadra Mustafa al-Sari (b. 1917) from Bir al-Maksur, District of Haifa, on Sept. 5, 1998; field researcher Muna Mahajneh.
2 Interview with Shams al-Taity (b. 1919) from al-'Aroub Camp, District of Khalil, on Nov. 8, 1998; field researcher Lamia' Shalalda.

*They knew nothing about politics or anything. No one ever saw them. They used to harvest and head home. We weren't open-minded like nowadays.*³

However, when the narrator felt more comfortable and ready to open her heart and mind, to set tradition aside, she would elaborate, and then her active participation in the struggle is revealed. This aspect of her role has been long denied. It sheds light not only on her individual contribution but also on the role of many rural women at that time.

In an interview with Khadra Mustafa al-Sari, she first insisted that women were not interested in anything but farming.

Interviewer: *Tell us about the women at that time.*
Khadra: *The women? In the cities, they were in the Black Hand group.*⁴ *The girls would carry baskets; that was in Haifa. The women and the girls would take food and water and go up the mountains.*
Interviewer: *What did they do exactly?*
Khadra: *They would go with the Black Hand group.*
Interviewer: *Did they fight with them or just go along?*
Khadra: *No, they were into it, tied to them [the young men]. We would aim and fire at a certain place.*
Interviewer: *And did they participate in the firing of weapons with the men?*
Khadra: *No, they'd go along at the ready. No one knows them. Whenever something happens, they know about it. They'd throw guns, take guns, put them in the baskets and cover them with greens.*⁵

After limiting the role of women to food and water, the narrator Shams al-Taity answers the researcher's question about women and their political work by saying: "Hamida Abu Rayya would fill the baskets with weapons, carry the weapons and set out, the soldiers would

---
3 Interview with Hamida Abu Rayya (b. 1922) from Samu', District of Khalil, on Nov. 20, 1998; field researcher Lamia' Shalaldeh.
4 The Black Hand (al-Kaf al-aswad) was an anti-Zionist and anti-British jihadist militant organization in mandatory Palestine. It was founded in 1930 by Syrian-born Sheikh Izz al-Din al-Qassam, who led it until his death. http://en.wikipedia.org/wiki/Black_Hand_(Mandatory_Palestine).
5 Interview with Khadra Mustafa al-Sari.

be standing at the gates, and she'd pass through, with baskets full of weapons; that was at the time of the British."[6] Even though she also understated the political role of women, the narrator Hamida Abu Rayya is a typical example of such participation, according to her own testimony and the testimonies of other women.

Through the research, it became apparent that Palestinian women have made major contributions to political life, both in the city and in rural areas. While the role of urban woman focused on political activism, the role of urban women focused on militant activity.

The Political Participation of Women in the 1940s

The research revealed how extensive the political participation of Palestinian women in the 1940s was (Abdulhadi 2006b). Despite the decline in their prominent role in armed struggle, rural women maintained their organic political participation, acting as a liaison among revolutionaries and transferring messages and important information. They also sustained their roles as instigators, drawing attention to the dangers of selling land, and continued challenging and clashing with the British forces and defending the villages attacked by the Zionist gangs. Meanwhile, urban women focused on the social work connected with political activism—a type of cultural work, which was closely connected with politics. They participated in politics through non-organizational public protests, such as their extensive participation in mass demonstrations and boycotts of foreign goods. They also made remarkable contributions to field hospitals serving the wounded.

During this decade, active women's associations and unions emerged, assuming various roles. In all cases, however, they were politically concerned, whether directly or indirectly. The associations were primarily involved in teaching, rehabilitating girls socially, and raising political awareness, by means of sewing, embroidery, and literacy courses, organizing political and educational lectures, and first aid training—which qualified some girls for working in field hospitals.

The research explored the role of the Chrysanthemum Flowers Society, revealing the notable militant and political activities of its female members, who were engaged in militant work as well as nursing during the association's short lifespan. The Chrysanthemum

---

6 Interview with Shams al-Taity.

Flowers Society was not obscure, but its political and militant role was not very evident. The current research sought to fill in the gaps in its history.

At the beginning, the Chrysanthemum Flowers' activities were charitable, more like a social club. Later it evolved into organized militant work. The founder, Mahiba Khurshid, explained how this shift took place after she witnessed the death of an innocent Palestinian child with her own eyes.[7] The association got its name, which indicates life, beauty, and constancy, from a French book the founder had read—referring to the Scarlet Pimpernel of the French revolution. It also evokes the chrysanthemum flower found in many parts of Palestine, a flower with petals shaped like shells for which the city of Bethlehem is famous symbolizing the beauty and the freedom of nature.[8] It is also the Margaret Flower,[9] which has a long lifespan, another emblem and symbol for the militants; in English tradition, it stands for fraternity, sacrifice, and asceticism.[10]

The research was able to correct the names of the two founders: Mahiba Khurshid and Nariman Khurshid. There were contradictory references to the name of the organization's leader—sometimes referring to her as "Juhayna," and sometimes as "Arrabiya Khurshid" (Abu Ali 1975; al-Khalili 1977:78)—while one reference called her "Mahiba Khurshid" (al-Dajani 1989). The research also managed to discover the nature of the association's chief line of work, since there were conflicting descriptions of this as well. According to some references, it was a group of female nurses, whose members enlisted to accompany the revolutionaries and provide them with supplies and weapons (Abu Ali 1975:47). Other references describe it as a military troop, without further elaborating on its military role (al-Dajani 1989:166).

In terms of the social changes that came along with the political struggle of women, which started as early as the 1930s, a more visible presence of women and a rise in their role were observed,

---

7 Interview with Mahiba Khurshid (b. 1925), Egypt, on Oct. 25, 1998; field researcher Amal al-Agha.
8 Interview with Mahiba Khurshid.
9 The Margaret plant is one of two members of the Chrysanthemum family.
10 Interview with Nariman Khurshid (b. 1927), Egypt, on Aug. 26, 1998; field researcher Amal al-Agha.

despite the social rigidness which continued in the 1940s, especially in rural areas. The number of literate women increased, and families relying on girls as economic providers were a widespread phenomenon—which hindered the marriage of many of them. Some families were also keen on teaching their girls music, painting, sculpting, and dancing. Politically pioneering women started demanding women's rights, and invading some fields that had long been monopolized by men, like journalism, public speech, producing radio programs, writing and directing plays and other performances, presenting exhibitions, and giving political and social speeches. In this context, the increasing presence of active women—in the consciousness of the narrators—seemed organic and coherent with their presence in the political and social reality.

The Political Contribution of Women from the 1950s to the 1960s

Written records of the struggle of Palestinian women in the 1950s and the 1960s are extremely limited in content, despite the fact that for the first time in history, women were politically active in Arab parties (Abdulhadi 2009). The research investigated the role of Palestinian and Arab organizations and federations that specifically supported the role of Palestinian women and sought to maintain their identity and sense of belonging. Some of these organizations were highly visible outside the country, such as the Arab Palestinian Women's Union in Lebanon, founded in 1952; the Palestinian Women's Federation in Cairo, founded in 1963; and the Association of the Returnee in Syria, founded in 1963. The General Union of Palestinian Women was founded in Jerusalem in 1965, as one of the bases of the Palestinian Liberation Organization (itself founded in 1964).

The research revealed an increase in women's participation in political work in the 1950s. Immediately after the Displacement of 1948, social work became closely connected with political work, according to most female narrators, due to the types of activities they engaged in. While the social aspect prevailed over the political aspect after 1948, the latter gained a larger scope in women's work beginning in the mid 1950s, through associations, unions, federations, and political parties. Women's associations became more interested in social development to provide sources of livelihood. Instead of providing material support for the evicted, they opened more literacy classes, founded more nurseries and workshops for sewing, embroidery, and knitting, cared for the families of martyrs and detainees, and organized fundraising events organized by women's societies as well as charity exhibitions. They also paid more attention to the educational aspect, organizing lectures and political and social discussions.

While women's unions focused on social activities serving indirect political purposes, the parties made a clear connection between their political and social work. In their testimonies, all of the narrators confirmed women's active political participation in demonstrations beginning in the mid 1950s.

With the increasing number of educated women, women's cultural participation expanded and women's political participation increased. The areas of creative writing and journalism became more diverse; more women started presenting programs; and the number of cultural committees in clubs and women's associations increased, where women were not just participants, but also founders. In addition to the increasing contribution of laywomen in local journalism, women stood out as professional journalists.

Women maintained their political role by working in cultural-social clubs, founding cultural-political clubs, and developing their relationship with writing. Despite their diverse scope, politics was the tie connecting all activities. Some women participated in theatrical production, writing and direction, script writing, training, and developing women's work in journalism. After taking these activities up as a hobby, some women sought to pursue academic degrees in these fields. Women's radio work, which started in the early 1950s, continued and increased in the early 1960s, as it became the profession of many of them. Also many female political activists participated in radio work as a political activity, not a professional one. At another level, more women became interested in first-aid training because of its relation to social-medical work and military work, according to the narrators' testimony.

In the mid 1950s and early 1960s, the correlation between the military and the medical fields was sustained, as the military work gained momentum with the foundation of the Palestine Liberation

Organization (PLO)[11] in 1964. The role of women in organizing Arab political parties persisted; they continued working as members of the Communist Party and the Arab Socialist Ba'th Party, with a remarkable level of participation in the Arab nationalist movement beginning in the mid 1950s. Since the 1960s, and after the foundation of the PLO in 1964, Palestinian women have participated in the women's movement within the Palestine Liberation Front.[12] A Women's Committee was also established within the Palestinian National Liberation Movement (Fatah) when the latter was founded in 1965, according to the narrators' testimonies.

One of the research objectives was to examine the organizational affiliation of Palestinian women with Arab political parties. Previous researchers noticed familial relations among the titles of active female party members and male politicians. This led to the conclusion that women's membership in these parties was driven by kinship rather than ideological conviction. According to the testimonies of several female narrators in the current research, their ideological affiliations with the parties were separate from the affiliations of their brothers, fathers, uncles, or husbands. However, they did not deny being influenced by the ideas discussed in family gatherings.

In her testimony, the narrator Nawal Hassan Hashishu confirms that she chose to marry someone who shared the same ideas and political affiliation, saying that she met her husband after becoming a member in the Arab Nationalist Movement. "The most important thing I had in mind was that if I were to marry, it would be to someone who shares the same line of thought, like me."[13] The testimony of the narrator Suhaila Yassin Abu

---

11 The Palestine Liberation Organization (PLO) is a political organization, recognized by the United Nations and the Arab League as the only legitimate representative of the Palestinian people inside and outside Palestine. It was founded in 1964 after the First Arab Palestinian Council in Jerusalem, as a result of the Arab League's resolution in its first summit meeting in Cairo in 1964, to represent the Palestinians internationally.

12 Ahmed Jibril founded the Palestine Liberation Front in 1959, and it initially enjoyed Syrian support. In 1967, the Front merged with the Heroes of Return (affiliated with the Arab Nationalist Movement) and the Young Avengers, forming the Popular Front for the Liberation of Palestine. In 1968, Jibril split from the Popular Front to form the Popular Front for the Liberation of Palestine–General Command.

13 Interview with Nawal Hassan Hashishu (b. 1937), Amman, Jordan, on March 1, 1999; field researcher Ruqaya al-'Alami.

Rishah similarly shows that she joined the Arab Socialist Ba'th Party as early as 1947, before meeting her husband, 'Abd Allah al-Rimawy, a party leader, and it also shows the narrator's leading position and personality.

The Role of Palestinian Women from the Mid 1960s to 1982

The research explored the participation of Palestinian women in the armed Palestinian Revolution since 1965; their foundational work in the National Palestinian Front in 1970; their prominent role in the First Palestinian Uprising (the First Intifada) in 1978; their work in establishing pioneer feminist frameworks in the late 1970s; and the role of the General Union of Palestinian Women from its foundation in 1965 to the Beirut Invasion in 1982 (Abdulhadi 2015). Fifty oral interviews were conducted with women who played a prominent role in the politics of 1965–82, or those who witnessed women playing a prominent political role during that time. The women were classified into two age groups: women older than 60 years, and women older than 50 but younger than 60 years, who witnessed the period from the mid 1950s to 1982. They were selected from Palestine (the West Bank, Gaza Strip, the 1948 areas, and Jerusalem), and from the diaspora in Jordan, Syria, Lebanon, and Egypt. The interviews also covered Palestinian cities, villages, and camps.

The narrators' testimonies reveal how early the Palestinian women engaged in Palestinian militancy by joining the Palestine Liberation Army. From 1965 to 1967, women's participation in demonstrations continued, chiefly against the Jordanian government. They protested against the detention of national activists and government policies such as Habib Bourguiba's visit to Jordan in 1965, and the events following the Samu' massacre. The narrators' testimonies point out the active academic and political role of female teachers and students during that historical period. They took part in printing and distributing leaflets, and the number of women participating in other kinds of political work and joining political parties increased.

The political participation of Palestinian women witnessed a surge after the Palestinian Revolution in 1965, with an increased involvement in their work within the armed resistance groups. This participation brought tangible social changes, as more women joined the military line of work. The cause of women, however, was never put forward as an independent cause, and the priority remained with militant work—despite the fact that some Palestinian factions acknowledged the importance of social change and adopted progressive slogans that depicted women as partners in the liberation battle.

The narrators pointed out the nature of the dominant social notions at that time, which resulted from a conservative and closed society. They talked about the difficulties they faced and that they were determined to confront and challenge. The women talked about how they were discriminated against; treated as people who needed to be under the permanent guardianship of men; forbidden to work, choose their partners, and leave the house except for emergencies; their work was limited to certain jobs and their potential was underestimated.[14] Describing the social changes that occurred after 1967, some narrators mentioned a decrease in dowries, an increased interest in education, the strengthening of social relations, the singing of national songs on various social occasions, and resorting to early marriage by some families.[15]

The political work at the time required both genders to carry out the necessary tasks, entrenching an image of women as partners, not subordinates. The narrator 'Abla Abu 'Ilba talked about the impact of the cooperation between young men and women in political work, and how it dictated a different style of life:

From day one, there were regular mixed meetings . . . including boys and girls, the person in charge could be a man or woman, so we didn't care much who was in charge, as long as the person was competent. Demonstrations were mixed, meetings were mixed, and there were educating meetings in the barracks[16] of al-Husain camp, which were also mixed, and educating meetings where we not only studied the national Palestinian cause, but also new ideologies, Marxism–Leninism, and the experiences of world revolutions in Vietnam, China and Latin America. . . .

---

14 Interview with Rashida 'Abd al-Hamid 'Ubaidu (b. 1947), Amman, Jordan, on Aug. 11 and Sept. 3, 2011; field researcher Mona Ghawsha.
15 Interview with Khadija Abu 'Arkub (b. 1943), Dora, Khalil, on Aug. 1, 2011; field researcher Lamia' Shalalda.
16 Houses with metal ceilings.

All this ... was joint work. I never ever found difficulty in dealing with this atmosphere. It was a very natural atmosphere, because the general values and nationalism ... were above all considerations.[17]

Through their political work, women challenged and refused the notions of shame, disgrace, and inferiority associated with their gender.[18]

The impact of their participation in military work reflected a partial change in the view of the nature of women's work and ability. The narrator 'Aisha Jabir Na'im talked about how the military operation she executed in 1969 changed her family's view of her work, replacing the sense of disgrace with a sense of pride.[19]

The women's testimonies show the impact of the 1967 aggression on the west bank of the Jordan River, the Gaza Strip, Sinai, and Golan; these events prompted an increase in the number of Palestinian women joining in political and military action. Women participated in political demonstrations, carried messages and weapons, wrote and distributed political leaflets, worked in secret commando groups (Fedayeen), provided the evicted with supplies, and helped the families of the martyrs and the detainees.

According to some female narrators, after the 1967 war, women were instigators in urging the people not to migrate. Moreover, they were active in the movement to boycott Israeli goods immediately after the occupation, and in demonstrations. They were also efficient participants in the teachers' strike, seeing it as an effective weapon of peaceful and popular resistance. The female narrators mentioned that after 1967 women were trained to carry weapons, did organizational work, studied nursing, and took first-aid field courses. Women were determined to take part in fighting all kinds of Israeli aggressions on Palestinian or Arab lands, by all possible means. In the Battle of Karameh in particular,[20] women carried out political and organizational tasks, acting as liaisons and nurses. After 1967, women were active participants in

---

17 Interview with 'Abla Abu 'Ilba (b. 1950), Amman, Jordan, on Aug. 29 and Sept. 9, 2011; field researcher Mona Ghousha.
18 Interview with 'Abla Abu 'Ilba.
19 Interview with 'Aisha Jabir Na'im (b. 1950), Damascus, Syria, on Nov. 5, 2011; field researcher Hala al-Ahmed.
20 The Battle of Karameh took place on March 21, 1968, when the Israeli army attempted to occupy the east bank of the Jordan River.

militant work—especially in the Gaza Strip—thanks to the military training classes the girls had taken in Gaza before, which helped qualify them for military work after the 1967 aggression.

After 1969, women's participation in military work increased, as more of them joined the Palestinian armed resistance groups. According to the female narrators, the parallel increase in women's political participation was influenced by their enlistment in armed resistance groups, especially in camps. Some narrators talked about the social transformation caused by the Palestinian armed activity, which reflected on the lives of camp residents, and the deep sense of identity they derived from this transformation. In addition to military training, women took part in leading training camps, transferring weapons, guarding locations, and executing military operations. With the increase of women's active organizational work, their involvement in Palestinian armed groups and Palestinian and Arab political parties also increased.

Palestinian women also continued their social-political work, within the general frameworks and structures of women in syndicates. They took to feminist work in connection with political work, forming popular feminist committees as well as feminist centers. They served in the field as medical responders, liaisons, and patrollers; led political demonstrations and sit-ins; worked in the cultural field, including radio and other media; wrote political statements and petitions; and helped raise funds. During armed battles, they formed relief groups, in addition to their communications and broadcasting work.

As members of the General Union of Palestinian Women, women pursued their feminist syndicate work—in addition to their general syndicate work—as they co-founded the General Union of Palestinian Teachers and continued to serve in the General Union of Palestinian Writers, the General Union of Palestinian Students, and the Palestinian Red Crescent agencies. They contributed to the General Union of Palestinian Doctors, helped found the Palestinian Doctors Union in Egypt, and were members of the preliminary committee of the latter union.

During this same period, Palestinian women also played a remarkable cultural role. This role was manifested in volunteer committees, and was carried out through charity associations, syndicate unions, and political groups. The notion of cultural work gained greater importance in the testimonies of the female narrators about this period; they demonstrated a deeper understanding of culture and its role, in close connection with politics. Women also had several media functions within their syndicates' frames, including celebrating special political occasions, forming artistic groups, writing media releases, organizing political discussions and conferences, and participating in local, Arab, and international conferences. Women's work in radio developed in parallel with their political participation. During that time, the fact that radio women belonged to resistance groups led to the politicization of the radio shows they produced or presented. According to narrators' testimonies, in this era there was an increase in women's participation in political demonstrations, which were associated with sit-ins, as several women explain.

Other Palestinian feminist associations were founded in the 1970s and 1980s. The Islamic Charity Association for Women was founded in 1974 as a social association with no political activity.[21] Kamila Nayef al-Mady reports: "The Women of Umm al-Fahem Association was founded in 1984—especially after the split of the Abna' al-Balad Movement (Children of the Homeland) in 1983, which largely affected the strength of the feminist movement. It was founded by al-Ansar, a breakaway movement which split from Abna' al-Balad."[22] The association's activity focused on establishing model nurseries and organizing exhibitions and cultural events.

In the late 1970s, the women's wings of the large organizations working under the PLO umbrella provided a feminist framework. Their main target was the political organization of women, through strengthening ties with the masses of women. The organizers tried to reach them in the factories, the fields, and their residences in villages, cities, and camps. Many women joined these frameworks, paving the way for broad participation by women in the First Intifada, starting on Dec. 9, 1987.

From the late 1970s to the mid 1980s, the political participation of Palestinian women accumulated, with an increased awareness of the necessary connection between social and political struggles, in order to maintain the gains of women and incur a radical social change. They were well aware of the difficulty of the social and political struggle, but because

---

21 Interview with Kamila Nayef al-Mady (b. 1942), Kafr Yasif, on Sept. 12, 2011; field researcher Ranin Jiryes.
22 Interview with Lubna Fawzy Ighbariya, Mahajina (b. 1959), Umm al-Fahm, on Jan. 22, 2012; field researcher Ranin Jiryis.

of their increasing participation in military work, "women became stronger, more robust, and braver, and they had feelings of pride and vigor. Women acquired more courage and an ability to face difficulties and find solutions to the problems they encountered."[23] Because of this development in the personality of Palestinian women, and the power and vigor they acquired, they became able to challenge, confront, and rebel against the social restrictions that limited their ability to contribute politically.

References
Abdulhadi, Faiha. 2006a. *The Political Participation of Palestinian Women in the 1930s*. Ramallah: Palestinian Women's Research and Documentation Centre.
———. 2006b. *The Political Role of Palestinian Women in the 1940s*. Ramallah: Palestinian Women's Research and Documentation Centre.
———. 2009. *The Political Role of Palestinian Women in the 50s until mid-1960s*. Ramallah: Palestinian Women's Research and Documentation Centre.
———. 2015. *The Political Role of Palestinian Women since 1965 until 1982*. Ramallah: Palestinian Women's Research and Documentation Centre.
Abu Ali, Khadija. 1975. *Introduction to the Women and Their Role in the Palestinian Revolt*. Beirut: General Union of Palestinian Women.
Anderson, K., S. Armitage, D. Jack, and J. Wittner. 1987. "Beginning Where We Are: Feminist Methodology in Oral History," *Oral History Review*, 15: 103–127.
al-Dajani, Ahmad Zaki. 1989. *Our City Jaffa and the 1936 Revolt*. Cairo: n.p.
Elsadda, Hoda. 1999. "How to Make Use of Feminist Literature in History Writing." In Faiha Abdulhadi, ed. *The Palestinian Women and Memory*, 160–168. Ramallah: Directorate of Gender/Ministry of Planning and International Cooperation.
Gluch, Sherna Berger, and Daghne Patai, eds. 1991. *Women's Words: The Feminist Practice of Oral History*. New York and London: Routledge.
al-Khalili, Ghazi. 1977. *Palestinian Women and the Revolution*. Beirut: PLO Research Centre.

---

23 Interview with Kamila Nayef al-Mady.

Mughanam, Metil. 1986. "Al-Gothoor al-tarikhiya li kefah al-mar'a al-filistiniya fil-haraka al-wataniya monthu al-intidab hatta 1936," *Samed al-Iqtisadi*, 62: 8–24.
Sayegh, Rosemary. 1980. *The Palestinian Farmers: From Expulsion to Revolution*. Beirut: Arab Research Institute.
al-Shihabi, Ibrahim Yahya. 1994. *The Village of Lubia*. Palestinian Demolished Villages Series 17. Birzeit: Birzeit University–Centre for the Documentation and Study of Palestinian Society.
Tonkin, Elizabeth. 1995. *Narrating Our Pasts: The Social Construction of Oral History*. Cambridge: Cambridge University Press.

II

Intersections:
Alternative Fields of History

CHAPTER 5

Memory, Memoir, and Oral History

Jean Said Makdisi

David Ben Gurion has been widely quoted as saying of the Palestinian refugees after 1948: "The old will die, and the young will forget." The old have indeed been dying, but the young have not forgotten; in fact, many young Palestinians who have never even seen Palestine claim to remember it. The question arises: how can you remember something you never knew? In the Palestinian case, there is no answer to the question, just a reiteration of the extraordinary truth that millions of people do. Memory, indeed, is the heart and soul of the Palestine struggle.

This chapter is not about Palestinian history but about some of the ways in which it, and its ramifications, such as the war in Lebanon, are remembered, and about the forms that embody the memory. In recent years oral history has become perhaps the most vibrant and useful instrument of probing and expressing this public memory. In 1979 Alessandro Portelli, one of the first theorists of oral history, identified memory as one of the elements that made oral history "'intrinsically different' from other historical sources" (quoted in Abrams 2010:19). But memoirs and autobiographies are other, often equally important instruments. I wish in this chapter to address both these forms in the Palestinian context.

First I would like to raise some questions: Can oral history, memoir and autobiography be considered complementary to one another, or is one by definition more significant than the other? Can a quirky, almost eccentric memoir written by a politically marginal individual cast a light on history that is of any value? Is the value of a memoir determined by the status of the writer, by his or her social standing? Is it determined by the nature and quality of the writing? Is the private memory of an individual woman in any way comparable as a meaningful historical source to the memoirs of a politically powerful man?

In the course of this presentation I shall address some of these questions based first on my own experience as a memoirist in *Beirut Fragments: A War* and *Teta, Mother and Me: Three Generations of Arab Women*, as editor of a memoir written by Serene Husseini Shahid, published as *Jerusalem Memories*, and as one of the editors of the English translation of the autobiography of Shafiq al-Hout, *My Life in the PLO: The Inside Story of the Palestinian Struggle*. I shall briefly compare these with each other and then with the formal work of oral history of one of the most traumatic experiences of our time: Bayan Nouwayed al-Hout's book *Sabra and Shatila: September 1982*. I shall also take a brief look at parts of the vast output of the oral historian Rosemary Sayigh, particularly the digital book *Voices: Palestinian Women Narrate Displacement*.

Theorists of oral history contrast it with memoir and autobiography, claiming that oral history is characteristically a creative, interactive process between interviewer and interviewee, while memoir and autobiography are, in their origins and their authority, basically unmediated. In her book on oral history theory Lynn Abrams writes that the critical distinction between oral history and autobiography

> is the involvement of the interviewer. . . . The story to be told may exist independently of the interviewer but the way it is expressed is influenced by the interviewer's intervention. Though there may be influences from editors or publishers, in a conventional written autobiography the initiative stays with the autobiographer from the first decision to narrate a life to what to include and exclude, how to shape the story and so on. Unlike storytelling or even middle-class autobiography . . . the narrator in an oral history interview gains the legitimacy to speak from the interviewer. (Abrams 2010:26–27)

The basic argument of oral historians is not so much with autobiography or memoir as it is with the documentary evidence on which historians tend to rely. We all know that personal memory is fallible, and to a certain degree unreliable, but Abrams points out that even such relied-upon historical sources as minutes of official meetings, accounts by journalists, and all other documents of history—including biographies, autobiographies, memoirs of important people—all rely to one degree or another on memory, and are all therefore subject to doubt as to their reliability.

My need to write what became my war memoir, *Beirut Fragments*, arose when I began to feel strongly that whatever was being written about the Lebanese war in the national and foreign press, as well as the many books that appeared during this period, often seemed unrelated to, or contradicted by, the experiences of ordinary people. The official record, based mostly on the words and actions of political and militia leaders on all sides, and on the accounts of media outlets over which they had major influence, or on members of the foreign press whose ignorance of the nuances of local politics was constantly decried by the Lebanese and Palestinian public, was belied by the many who questioned, debated, mocked, and sometimes angrily denounced those same leaders, whether on their own side or the others, as liars and malefactors interested only in their personal power and interests. This led me to question whether accepted history, based on official documents, official statements, and press reports, was more valuable than individual experience.

I began to write the voices of those, including myself and my family, colleagues at university, and countless others, whose stories circulated or were deliberately told to me as witness to the savagery and inherent injustice of war. I felt it my business to counter the official narrative with that of those who were being ignored, not only by the local and international power structures, but by the local and international press as well. The odious phrase "the silent majority" (coined by the former US vice president Spiro Agnew) was used a great deal in those days, and often by those who terrorized the majority and then claimed to speak in its name. I meant to undo the very notion of public silence, and to that degree my writing was intentionally subversive. The nature of the experiences I wrote about was of course not reducible to a single quality: many were tragic, some comic; some were banal and others fraught with meaning; some predictable and others surprising. And it was precisely the variety of human experience which interested me, and which I saw as a civilized counterweight to the war.

Later, when I worked on my second book, *Teta, Mother and Me: Three Generations of Arab Women* (2005), I had a similar experience. Our three generations covered more than a hundred years in Syria, Palestine, Egypt, and Lebanon, but the formal history of the period entirely left out the experiences of women. I found this particularly surprising in light of the vast cultural changes, most of which fell well into the space of female authority and domestic life, that took place during my grandmother's youth, when the Levant was transformed from a corner of the vast Ottoman Empire into a group of small countries dominated by western imperial powers. Languages, schools, costume, food, songs, interiors—all these and much more were transformed to a large extent in the domestic sphere.

In the absence of a formal history I could count on to help reconstruct or at least provide a suitable background for the life of my grandmother, about whom I found I had very little tangible knowledge, I had to rely almost entirely on interviews, letters, diaries, and memoirs—especially ones written at my request by my mother and her brothers. Aside from these memoirs, a few family letters, a book of school records, and some interviews with the few surviving women who had known her in her lifetime were my only sources of knowledge of my grandmother's life and the early life of my mother. My task gradually became not just to honor my mother and grandmother, as I had set out to do, not just to trace the trajectory of my cultural heritage as an Arab woman, but also to place us and our ordinary lives on the public record.

While still engaged in my work on *Teta, Mother and Me*, I began editing the memoirs of Serene Husseini Shahid, an elderly Palestinian woman from a notable Jerusalem family, now living in Beirut. When she first came to see me, she carried with her a handwritten series of anecdotes and memories mostly about her early life in pre-catastrophe Palestine, and shyly asked my opinion as to whether or not they were worth pursuing. Hers was a formless collection, written in no order but that dictated by the whims of random thoughts and glimpses of memory. They were also written in English, and though the language was correct it was devoid of character and of idiomatic fluency. She had chosen to write in English as a political device, for she wished "them," as she called the outside world, to know about the reality of a historic Arab presence in Palestine, and because she felt the need to preserve and transmit the memory of this presence as she had embodied and experienced it.[1]

At the time, and before and since, the question of Palestine had been endlessly discussed, debated, and documented. Thousands of books had been written on, and many journals were dedicated to, the subject, to which I used irritably to refer as "the Palestine industry." Professional historians, journalists, novelists, poets, filmmakers, artists, and activists—not to mention politicians—were actively engaged in recording, elucidating, and explaining the Palestinian experience, and arguing the justice of the cause. Mostly, though certainly not exclusively, this body of work was—and still is—dominated by men, as were all political decisions. It was easy for individuals, especially I think women, to feel frustrated, isolated, and alienated from this deluge of production, and to feel utterly left out and voiceless. I had felt this myself many times, and with it the need to carve my existence into a tiny corner of our history, from which I had been—or at least had felt myself to have been—excluded, for a variety of reasons.

Because I sympathized with her situation and motives, I encouraged Serene to continue her efforts, and promised I would try to help. Several people to whom I turned on her behalf for advice thought the anecdotes—often without reading them—uninteresting, banal, and insignificant. These were the intimate memories of an upper-class, elderly woman, totally unrepresentative of the vast majority of Palestinians, and therefore worthless. One person engaged in the Palestine struggle even went so far as to tell me that, as they were the product of a particular family, they had nothing to contribute to the struggle, and were even ideologically objectionable.

As I was at the time working on my own book, I tried to help Serene find a professional editor who could take on the job of working on these small autobiographical pieces—most of them were barely two or three pages long—to make them more fit for publication. But those to whom we sent the papers seemed to want to convert them—I should say to *elevate* them—into a formal history of a family and a nation, and thus, though ruining their character, make them an acceptable component of the body of Palestinian political literature.

---

[1] For a longer look at many such individual memoirs written by Palestinian women in English, see Jean Said Makdisi 2010.

In my view, however, the value of these anecdotes was precisely in their recording the memories of a Palestinian girlhood—for if children's lives are rarely recorded in Arab histories, the lives of girls are even less so. The politics of Palestine, the British occupation, the Zionist colonization, the political and military activities of the resistance movement against both the British and the Zionists—in short, all the momentous aspects of modern Palestinian history—were inevitably present in the anecdotes. After all, several of Serene's male relations, including her father, Jamal al-Husseini, his cousin Hajj Amin al-Husseini, and her maternal uncle Musa al-Alami, were directly involved in Palestinian politics. (At the time she was writing her memories her daughter was involved as well, acquiring fame as an exceptionally articulate spokeswoman for the Palestinian government.) Arrests, banishments and exile, clashes with the British as well as with the Zionists, are peppered throughout her stories. Thus she recorded some of the important moments of modern history, though from an oblique and entirely personal perspective, and not in the straightforward expository form normally expected in memoirs.

One of her stories, for instance, recounts an event which occurred during the 1936 revolution in Palestine. A crop of eggplants had been planted as an investment on a piece of land owned jointly by her father and his brother-in-law Musa al-Alami. As the general strike dragged on the eggplants ripened, but could not be harvested or taken to market, so they began to spoil on the branch. To save the crop, her father decided to collect the eggplants and pickle them in tins that would be ready for sale once the strike ended. He insisted that the best place to store the tins was in the basement of the family home in Jerusalem, where, as Alami protested, the latter's father's books, including copies of an important index to the Qur'an, were also stored. So pickled eggplants and the Qur'anic index were placed together in the basement, until disaster struck. Peering down into the basement one afternoon, Alami found that the pickles had fermented, burst their containers, and floated on the floor along with the remnants of the books. Thus both the investment and the books were ruined (Shahid 2000:95–103).

Other incidents seem even more irrelevant, quite individual. Serene describes, for instance, the day when as a tiny child she was first presented at table with a bowl of jelly, the quivering red mound placed in front of her in the house of American friends of the family in the American Colony in Jerusalem. Totally alarmed by the wobbly nature of the jelly, she had no idea what to do with it, until she was instructed to eat and enjoy it, which she most emphatically did not. I found in this story not merely an amusing anecdote but a reminder of the kind of cultural exchange that habitually took place in pre-1948 Palestine.

I likened the form created by Serene to miniature naive paintings, illustrating the pre-1948 physical, political, and social landscape of Palestine, as well as aspects of the Palestinian experience in exile.

An important aspect of her memories was that many of them take place against an intimately known and comfortingly unified geographical background which I found deeply moving. "I have discovered," she writes in one of the early pieces, "that my happiest recollections are of places rather than people. After all, people die and take away part of us with them, while places live forever. So I close my eyes and go to Jericho in winter, Sharafat in summer, and Jerusalem in spring" (Shahid 2000:21).

Jerusalem neighborhoods, from Musrara to Sheikh Jarrah, the ancient alleys of the old city, the American Colony, the Maskobie and others; Ramallah, Beissan, Sharafat, Jericho—as well as architectural notes of the many family houses and their physical settings—all come alive in her little stories, reawakening the memory of a once unified landscape familiar to pre-1948 Palestinians, but since fragmented and defaced by the bloody history of colonialism, occupation and war. (In an interesting study of aboriginal memory as it applies to the physical landscape of Australia, Maria Nugent (2008) uses a term, 'geo-biography,' to designate the way in which places that have acquired significance in the present—i.e., 'post-contact' Australia[2]—are invested with meaning relevant to 'pre-contact' life, when aboriginal ownership of the land and proprietorial comfort in it was unchallenged. It seems to me that parallels can be drawn between Australian Aboriginal and Palestinian landscapes respectively as they affected the personal and public memories of the victims of colonialism, and their collective sense of loss and oppression.)

---

2   The terms 'pre-' and 'post-contact' in Nugent's paper refer to the first contact in 1770 with the European colonialists, when Captain Cook first "discovered" Australia. From an aboriginal perspective it is the date of loss and national tragedy, very similar to the Palestinian 1948 and its own term, the *nakba*.

Angered by the suggestion that some voices were to be excluded from the historical record for the ideological reasons I have mentioned, and feeling strongly that a Palestinian woman's memories of daily life in the 1920s, 1930s, and 1940s, however insignificant in themselves, were of value to this larger picture, I decided to take up the task of editing them myself. I saw my main task as editor as probing Serene's failing memory, Anglicizing her English, researching the facts, and perhaps above all providing a coherent narrative framework for the isolated and unrelated incidents that she recorded. As I worked, I believe I played a role not unlike that of the oral historian who helps shape the narrative of a lost past retrieved by memory.

A few years after Serene's book, with an introduction by Edward Said, was published, I worked on the English translation of Shafiq al-Hout's memoir, *My Life in the PLO: The Inside Story of the Palestinian Struggle*. Shafiq al-Hout was an important figure in the modern history of the Palestinian struggle, especially in the context of the PLO's political and military presence in Lebanon. He chose to write about particular moments in his life from his huge store of political experience, including details of significant historic events in which he was directly involved. He provides fascinating insights into some of the movers of Palestinian and Arab history with whom he had personal relations, including such figures as Gamal Abdel Nasser, whom he greatly admired, King Hussein, and of course Yasser Arafat and many others. Yet in his book he meant to record as well his personal feelings, his emotions, and especially his great love for Palestine. His memories of childhood and schooldays in his beloved Jaffa, lost to and deeply mourned by him, are intensely nostalgic and moving.

My work with Shafik al-Hout's text involved problems of language and idiom inevitable in a translation, but one word in particular caused me much disquiet. This single word, or group of words, shows the degree to which individual memoir can call up and even embody the national culture which is the frame of reference for the individual memory. Lynn Abrams writes: "Memory is key to our identity; without our memory we have no social existence.... Without personal memory we are unable to satisfactorily construct a viable sense of self. Memory then is about the present as much as the past" (2010:82). All memories embodied in either memoir or oral history are expressed in a particular language, and thus personal experience is bound to that language. The group of words that made me so uneasy included *shahid, istishhad, istashhad,* and so on. *Akhi istashhad* translated into English is 'my brother was martyred' or, more pleasingly though not as correctly, 'became a martyr.' I had several discussions with Shafik al-Hout about this: while he insisted, and I acknowledged, that 'martyr' is unquestionably the correct translation of *shahid,* I still felt uncomfortable using it, feeling its incongruity in the context of the English language and its culture. I discussed the problem with several friends—scholars, poets, writers—whose language is Arabic, but who are also fluent in English. All insisted that the only possible translation of *shahid* is 'martyr,' and in the end I gave up my search for a more suitable word and surrendered to its use. Still, I remained uncomfortable with it. In Arabic, the word *shahid* has a very specific and very positive cultural meaning and connotation, while in English it sounds archaic, stilted, negative, even somehow unreal. In this part of the world we have all lived in the shadow of wars, occupations, and resistance movements, so for us the word *shahid* is not only quite natural and thoroughly unambiguous but also clearly political.[3] (Political argument, for instance, can be made as to whether or not the title should be rightfully bestowed on this or that individual). In English, however, the word 'martyr' calls up ancient images of early Christians being fed to lions, heretics being burned at the stake, and wars for political dominance between defenders of rival orthodoxies during and following the European Renaissance. I felt that its use would add to the orientalist perception of Arab culture with which we were confronted in our pursuit of justice.

Oral history theorists inquire to what degree individuals, whether consciously or unconsciously, depend in the formation of their memories on the national or collective culture (Abrams 2010:23). I think it important to note that language is involved in untangling the relationship between private, individual memory and the collective memory that in its turn depends on the individual, and eventually leads to the formation of a collective or national identity.

---

3 Following the horrific explosions in Burj al-Barajneh in Beirut on November 12, 2015, a reporter on one TV channel noted with indignation and anger the use by a rival channel of the word *qutala* ('those killed') instead of *shuhada* ('those martyred') for the victims of the operation, and saw in this diction an unacceptable political stance.

In Bayan Nuwayhed al-Hout's masterly work of oral history on the Sabra and Shatila massacres that took place in Beirut during the Israeli invasion of Lebanon in 1982, the historian probes individual memory with the purpose of creating a national one. As I read her introduction I was astonished to find that she felt compelled to begin the story not with the Israeli invasion that began three months before the massacres, or even with the Lebanese war that began in 1975, but with the First Zionist Congress convened by Theodor Herzl in Basel in 1897, almost a hundred years earlier. This diligence clearly indicates her desire to provide an unassailably legitimate historical background to the events of 1982. In this fascinating introduction, Bayan al-Hout takes up some theoretical and practical issues that framed her inquiry. The massacre became the focus of worldwide press attention, but as this attention faded, the Lebanese government took a decision to suppress all investigations into the matter, and "the slightest mention of the massacre was forbidden" (2004:8). It was at this point that Bayan decided to undertake her oral history project. "My sole aim . . . at this stage was to document and preserve testimonies in any way possible, for fear they should be lost, or else face the negative impact of proscription" (2004:8). Because the scene of the disaster was under constant surveillance, most of the interviews had to be done secretly in her own home or in the homes of friends.

If I were asked what remained most significantly in my memory, I should have to say it was the abnormally secret, even impossible atmosphere surrounding the whole affair. For instance, she had to make second copies of the recorded interviews. This procedure, she writes, is not a basic requirement of oral history, but given the worsening security situation it was essential: "keeping just the one [copy] would have been an unforgivable lapse" (2004:9).

It was not, however, until the Kahan Report, the Israeli Commission of Inquiry into the massacres, was published in February 1983 that a shocked, bitter, and angry Bayan al-Hout decided to work toward the publication of a book of oral history to set the record, so distorted by the Israeli report, straight. Her anger led her to rethink some of the decisions she had made earlier. Her first thought had been merely to record the tragic human experience. She had neglected, for instance, in her early zeal, to ask people for names of their murdered relatives.

I was . . . gazing into the depths of human tragedy. I would hardly, for example, interrupt a weeping mother to say "What's your daughter's name?". . . There was no way I felt I could ask such a question before the Kahan Report was issued. What difference did it make whether her daughter's name was Leila or Mariam? (al-Hout 2004:11)

Now, however, she decided to take a more precise and technical look at what had happened: specifically, she decided to count the bodies, and to name the victims. She describes her work and the massive difficulties that she faced. And she writes: "The really difficult part of all this was the conversion of human experience into numbers and percentages. Yet someone had to do it, in response to the misleading figures provided before" (2004:14).

At the beginning of the book Bayan al-Hout writes of "the essential difference between the historiography of massacres and that of other historical events." But why is this so? "Because massacres are, with rare exceptions, characterized by secrecy. Because massacres normally involve no documents or records" (2004:4). But most important of all, she writes:

Because massacres have known beginnings but no endings. . . . Those who survive do not live on like people truly alive . . . . Because the researcher of massacres constantly uncovers things previously unknown, even in the single story of a single family. Witnesses constantly remember more, telling in later meetings things they had not revealed at the start. (2004:4)

At the end of the book are the appendices: pages and pages of tables of the names of the victims, their ages, genders, next of kin, financial responsibilities within their families, their places of residence, their hometowns in Palestine, and more details. One table is particularly moving: she lists with each victim's name the number of times he or she had been displaced. There follow pages and pages of horrific photographs; pages and pages of sources and bibliography.

Bayan al-Hout's book is focused on meticulous truth-telling and record-keeping. Because of the political importance of her subject, she needed to produce an oral history of the massacre which could not be challenged on the basis of the slightest historical inaccuracy or methodological lapse. The amazing thing about the book is that, while being so technically sound, it never loses touch with the deeply emotional nature of the inquiry.

In her digital book, *Voices: Palestinian Women Narrate Displacement*, Rosemary Sayegh places at our disposal the voices of the women she interviewed in Gaza, the West Bank, 1948 Palestine, and Jerusalem. "The voices" here is meant literally, as the actual recordings of the interviews are reproduced on the website to great dramatic effect. The short written introductions to each story suddenly come to life as the individual interviewee blossoms into a real person, with distinctive idiosyncrasies of speech and voice. One sounds shy and close-lipped, another loud and assertive, yet another calm and collected. Some have rural accents and some urban; some speak in the refined Arabic of the middle class, others reflect a poorer background. Few novelists could achieve as sharply the sense of these characters that one knows only from their telling of their stories. Once again, we are reminded of the importance of language as it emphasizes, defines, and elaborates the nuances of personal memory in the context of public trauma. In all, the book provides a devastating collection of accounts, each separate and different from the others, but all in the end variations on the themes of terror, loss, violence, displacement, and personal tragedy.

Before her trip to Palestine in which these interviews were recorded, Sayegh had done much work probing memories of women in the Palestinian refugee camps in Lebanon. A horrific event during the sea flight from Haifa in 1948 is remembered by one of her respondents and put on the public record by Sayegh.

When we were in the middle of the sea, halfway to Beirut, we had a pregnant woman on board, she was in labor.... [M]y aunt, God have mercy on her soul, told her, "Come over here" and made her squat. And a baby was born and it was a boy. They had nothing to wrap him in. I had a bundle of things for my son, so I undid it and gave her some. There wasn't anything to cut the umbilical cord. My younger brother Isma'il had a piece of iron in his pocket. They took it from him and cut the cord. (Sayegh 1998:46)

In this story, the ultimate female experience occurs in the context of the exodus, and becomes a symbol not just of the suffering, but also of the survival, continuity, and solidarity of the community.

The work of the historian and that of the memoirist are entirely different. As memory takes different forms for different purposes and with different results, so should we have different approaches to its invocation. Bayan al-Hout's devastating reconstruction of the Sabra and Shatila massacres, and Rosemary Sayegh's heroic output of interviews and record-keeping, are important sources of knowledge of the history of Palestinians. Shafik al-Hout's memoirs are important as a political and historical document. Serene Husseini Shahid's delicate, even eccentric, little anecdotes are in no way analogous in importance to any of these, but still her voice adds a touch of color, childlike humor, and loving tenderness to the history of a people's tragedy, and its almost relentless record of loss, defeat, and denial.

There is, I am sure, much value in the retelling of the past in various mediums. With each variation in the recording of personal experience, an extra dimension is added to our perception of history.

References

Abrams, Lynn. 2010. *Oral History Theory*. London: Routledge.
al-Hout, Bayan Nouwayed. 2004. *Sabra and Shatila: September 1982*. London: Pluto Press.
al-Hout, Shafiq. 2011. *My Life in the PLO: The Inside Story of the Palestinian Struggle*. London: Pluto Press.
Makdisi, Jean Said. 1990. *Beirut Fragments: A War Memoir*. New York: Persea Books.
———. 2005. *Teta, Mother and Me: An Arab Woman's Memoir*. London: Saqi Books.
———. 2006. *Teta, Mother and Me: Three Generations of Arab Women*. New York: Norton.
———. 2010. "Representations: Memoirs, Autobiographies, and Biographies: Writing in Another Language: Palestinians Writing in English." In Suad Joseph, ed. *Encyclopedia of Women & Islamic Cultures* (*EWIC*). http://dx.doi.org/10.1163/1872-5309_ewic_EWICSIM_0665, accessed on January 12, 2018.

Nugent, Maria. 2008. "Mapping Memories: Oral History for Aboriginal Cultural Heritage in New South Wales, Australia." In Paula Hamilton and Linda Shopes, eds. *Oral History and Public Memories*, 47–64. Philadelphia: Temple University Press.

Sayigh, Rosemary. 1998. "Palestinian Camp Women as Tellers of History," *Journal of Palestine Studies*, 27/2(106): 42–58.

———. *Voices: Palestinian Women Narrate Displacement.* http://almashriq.hiof.no/voices/

Shahid, Serene Husseini. 2000. *Jerusalem Memories*. Beirut: Naufal.

CHAPTER 6

The Novel as a Repository for Oral and Women's History

Rafif Saidawy

Introduction

The supreme human ideals and the pursuit of perfection were and are still the dream of novelists and the base for every narrative work, despite the conviction that this perfection is impossible to attain. We have chosen to examine the novel as a repository of oral history because the history of this literary genre suggests that the advancement of the novel as an art has coincided with its rebellion against the Arab reality with all its negative aspects in an attempt to reach a better life. Characters clash with their societies, as manifested in the conflict between the ego and the outdated customs and traditions of the society, or between the ego and patriarchal society and justice, or between the ego and the subordination of this society to the power of money, status, and political influence.

Within this framework, Arab novels have struggled against all kinds of attacks on memory. These attacks can affect memories in various ways. Three of these forms were classified by Paul Ricoeur. The first is repressed memory (*mémoire empêchée*), which occurs when a person's memory suffers a shock or a trauma, often in the form of being "forced to face types of loss" and "forgetfulness" (*oublieuse*). The second is manipulated memory (*mémoire manipulée*), usually associated with a fragile identity, or with an encounter with the 'other' which poses a threat to it, or to the "ideologizing of memory" as manipulated by authorities to serve the official history, "framing the official tale to serve the group identity framing." Thirdly, forced memory (*mémoire obligée*) is imposed under the pretext of justice—for example, in claiming the right to enforce national reconciliation policies in democratic societies based on justice and equity, to recognize and remember the Other and his/her memory, and to pay the debt for the predecessors who made us who we are, including war and conflict victims whose remembrance is a patriotic and moral priority. When this third type of remembrance becomes a duty, one's own memory becomes the tool of selective memory (Ricoeur 2000:83–109, 585–589).

Arab narrative texts appear to be a sociological framework through which all sorts of Arab disorder and imbalance are exposed and debated. They also reflect an expressive framework of the self, or a collective memory conflict, against all the violations being perpetrated against it, so as to form an authentic memory rather than a distorted one. The Lebanese novelist Elias Khoury, for example, expresses his obsession with preserving what is hidden in the official Lebanese history:

> *I suddenly discovered that I was a man whose awareness of the civil war started with its introduction in 1968. I realized as well that this society had erased its history as if it were holding a huge eraser to erase its own history per se. The situation is that there is no text about the year 1860, the 20 Revolution or the 58 Revolution. The fearful moment is that I was living in a war (1975–) which may have the same fate as its predecessors. Hence, it was my obsession to write about it, and I started to search for memory formulation.* (Amir 1993:59)

The modern novel, like historiography, is a link between the past lived by the people of yesterday and the present time. The historical material of modern fiction is not confined to the facts per se, but is subordinated to the artistic structure embodying the logic of the novel and its creative vision. This is what makes the novel, as a human creation, capable of giving meaning to a particular historical experience, and of integrating the historical group into a single collective identity which is continually being narrated and interpreted.

The multiplicity of modern narrative styles, the narrative patterns of the Arabic novel, and the superiority of the novel to other literary genres in the ability to contain large-scale expressions of sociopolitical and cultural realities, allows the novelist considerable space for movement and expression. It also permits the use of a variety of narrative techniques.

Oral history is one of these narrative tools; its discourse often contests the dominant knowledge and ideologies, including cultural stereotypes of women in the past and the present. A number of narrative texts have documented the voices and testimonies of marginalized Arab women, whether in Classical Arabic or in the various colloquial forms, in order to establish new knowledge that is capable of changing awareness; the goal of this knowledge is to dislodge the formal memory or the ideologizing consciousness. The belief that a novel has the power to lead to change might be an exaggeration of its capabilities. Nevertheless, the Arabic novel has deconstructed the ground upon which the Arab political, social, and knowledge systems were based. This genre of narrative writing style is characterized by artistic creativity and possesses the tools that allow it to delve deeper into the social world from which the novelist produces his/her narrative world. In this sense, Arabic novels, though not directly initiating change, may foresee its potential direction through the production of alternative knowledge.

Oral History and Imagination

A few methodological remarks are in order.

First, every novel is necessarily a historical narrative because it expresses a certain historical view and carries a specific new perspective on it. Does this mean that a novel is not a 'real' text? This is a legitimate question since the factual references in the narrative text make the text itself appear to be factual. We may say that our reading of narrative text must take the literary structure into account, so that the function, boundaries, and role of oral history in the narrative structure are identified. Classifying the narrative text as history leads to two errors. The first is the separation of the historical material from its context, which gives the narrative text its character. As Paul Ricoeur states, the narrative plot is not static; it is a complementary process and procedure which cannot be completed unless the reader or the recipient of the story is engaged in it. The meaning or denotation of the narration springs from the interaction between the world of the text and the world of the reader (Ricoeur 1999:47). The second error is the projection of the qualities of honesty, credibility, truth, and the like, which are assumed for the historical material and which the reader tends to project into the imaginary texts. This means that the extent to which the story is credible and the necessity of credibility have to be considered. In this context, Paul Ricoeur's concept of the apparent contradiction between "a historical story" (or a historical book) and "fiction" (the novel, even the factually based novel) may be helpful. The two types of books differ with respect to the nature of the implicit understanding between the author and the reader. The novel's reader is being prepared to enter an unreal world where the requirement of knowing when, how, and where these things happened no longer exists. The reader enters the world of the narrative text, accepting this game as if the narrated events have really occurred. The reader of a history book or a historical text, in contrast, expects to join a world of events which really occurred. Consequently, the historical text should be read critically, as it is expected to present a truthful discourse with a great deal of scientific credibility (Ricoeur 2000:334–40). However, this duality resulting from the difference between the two references—i.e., the factual reference of the historical book and the imaginary reference of the narrative—disappears when the experience of real life constitutes a common ground upon which both types of books rely.

Second, building on the idea that oral history is embedded in narrative, this chapter examines specific novels as an oral archive maintaining the female memory against oppression, forgetfulness, and Ricoeur's distorted memory forms (repressed, manipulated, and forced), especially in patriarchal and dictatorial systems. The novel is "a reading of a historical or an imagined event which is narrated by multiple voices, and each voice expresses its own point of view whereas history is written in one voice (the voice of the historian which describes events from the authority's standpoint, in general). In this sense, the historical memory of the novel is richer and broader than that of history books" (Shahayid 2011:202). This chapter examines the ways in which a novel occupies a large part of the sociocultural reality in which it is engaged ideologically. This engagement is the subject of the social and the historical topic, especially because it reveals a range of internal relations in the society and the patterns among these relations.

In other words, the main focus of this research is the social function of remembering, particularly the remembering of women, based on the fact that the self—whether individual, collective, or communal—is the sum of what we remember. Any attempt to erase this memory becomes a strike directed to its heart. We do not simply recall or live memories, but most importantly we reconstruct them as well. However, this construction process faces several impediments, the most prominent of which is forgetfulness. The various forms and patterns of forgetfulness blocking the process are "often intentional, completed directly or indirectly. The more memories we exclude because they are disturbing or because we want to marginalize them, the more they sink into oblivion, but they never die" (Shahayid 2011:202).

This chapter describes the ways in which female memory was retrieved and saved from forgetfulness and loss. In addition to being "a way of thinking and living," culture in general is also "a memory" and "an identity." The importance of the selected texts lies in their "narrative identities," which fill the gaps in the collective consciousness by providing historical continuity for women. What is meant by narrative identity here is that which "is realized by time through narration" (Ricoeur 1999:29). This occurs because the "narrative identity" is

> *a conceptual issue which rests on survival in time, and through the linguistic tradition conveyed by narration [it becomes] a form of the self—not existence for one's own self but existence for others —with and among them in an uninterrupted movement of past, present and future acts transmitted by the present narrative heritage and the traditions which precede the actual existence of the self.* (Ricoeur 1999:29)

In the narrative context, resistance of forgetfulness is a form of social expression in the face of change. For example, the "Arab Spring" is a pivotal event in Arab history, but it has not yet generated any narrative, because the novel as a genre requires a time interval to separate it from the historical incident it represents, in order to present mature reflection on the subject. This chapter discusses two narrative texts published before and after the Arab Spring: *al-Tanturiya* (2010) by the Egyptian novelist Radwa Ashour, and *Tchari* (2013) by the Iraqi novelist In'am Kajji. The reasons for selecting these two works are, first, both novels represent the female perspective in their approach to the Arab reality. Another reason is that *al-Tanturiya*, although published before the Arab Spring, describes the mismanagement of the Palestinian cause and the tragedy of the Palestinian refugees, and thus foreshadows the change that was yet to come. *Tchari* was published during the Arab

Spring without addressing this period directly; however, its detailed description of the disintegration in Iraq reflects the events of that time. This is accomplished by recalling an oppositional memory regarding the difficulties in Iraq and perhaps in other Arab countries. Any work of literature is concerned with

> *proving, with or without an ideological consciousness, a particular policy which art cannot reject the temptation to address, especially since the link between the interpersonal (interindividuelles) imagination directly or indirectly requires a set of roles and a network of communal relations. Hence, ideology can, insofar as it represents a holistic example for these relations, be revealed in every cultural construction, allowing criticism a space to eliminate deception.* (Ansart 1974:17)

Al-Tanturiya: Palestine Seen through the Memory of Women's Struggle

Al-Tanturiya, by Radwa Ashour, depicts the epic of the Palestinian tragedy through the protagonist and narrator, who is in her seventies. Ruqayya was 15 years old when the 1948 Nakba ('Catastrophe') took place, involving massacres by Zionists in many Palestinian towns and villages, including Tantoura. Her memory intersects with the Palestinian collective memory. The novel is structured as a first-person narration by Ruqayya in response to the request of her son Hassan. She asks him, "Why have you entangled me in this writing? What sense does it make for me to live through the details of the disaster twice?" (Ashour 2014:183). He replies,

> *I got your letter. You say, what sense is there and what's the use? I say that I wanted others to hear your voice, the voice of Ruqayya the woman from Tantoura. Your four children, we know that voice because we were raised with it. We know you and we know that you have a lot to tell people. It's not only the story I'm interested in, I'm after the voice, because I know its value and I want others to have the chance to hear it.* (Ashour 2014:185)

This is how the female voice gained importance in historicizing more than 60 years (1936–2000) of the Palestinian catastrophe, as it was experienced in the family of the brothers Abu al-Sadeq and Abu al-Amin, the grandfathers from whom Ruqayya and her offspring descend: Ruqayya (Abu al-Sadeq's daughter), Amin (Abu al-Amin's son and Ruqayya's husband), their sons' generation, and their grandchildren's generation.

Despite the fact that this voice—the voice of the female—expresses the novelist/narrator's viewpoint of this tragedy, the story does not exclusively center on Palestinian women's history. However, the voice describes all the levels of the tragedy that the text of *al-Tanturiya* covers, attempting to revive and restructure the collective memory without ignoring the historicization of Palestinian women's society all through the narrative. Ruqayya's voice predominates over other voices in the story, so that the narrator dominates the writing throughout the book, even though the history is also presented by the narrative memories of other characters. This dominance is symbolized by the role of women as home-keepers: they carry the keys of the homes they inherited from their mothers, and they never lose the hope of returning one day to those homes. Years later, according to Ruqayya, "when we moved to Beirut and I participated in the campaign for literacy among women in Shatila, . . . I had to visit the women of the camp to convince them of the importance of literacy. I discovered that what I had inherited from my mother was common. I found it strange—how could the women all do the same thing, without any prior agreement?" (Ashour 2014:74).

The key of Abu al-Sadeq's house was passed to Ruqayya by her mother; Ruqayya eventually gives it to her granddaughter, Little Ruqayya. Like her mother, Ruqayya never takes off the key, even to bathe (Ashour 2014:285). She reports:

> *I was met by Umm Ibrahim, an elderly woman in her sixties . . . . She said, "We're from Saasaa, do you know it? . . . She continued, telling me about it and about the two massacres that occurred there. . . . Umm Ibrahim put her hand to her breast and showed me the key suspended on a cord around her neck. She said, "The key to our house." . . . Later on I would learn that most of the women of the camp carried the keys to their houses, just as my mother did.* (Ashour 2014:74)

Palestine in the Voice of Women

When we strive to rebuild the past, it is founded on the present, "the memories of others and the great frameworks of the society's memory"

(Halbwachs 2012:35). Moreover, the "succession of memories, even the most subjective, is always explained by the changes in our relationships in the different social milieus, i.e., the transformations of these milieus, whether for each individual or as a whole" (Halbwachs 1997:95). Conversely, the fact that this history depends on the written archive—articles, reports, letters, maps, and the like—does not deny the dependence of *al-Tanturiya* on oral transmission. The stories, songs, musical compositions, folk proverbs, and other elements of the oral heritage that make up the public oral history are all focused on the memories of the narrative characters.

The memories of these characters are deconstructed into geographically based collective memories of Palestinian society. While Ruqayya's memory depends on Tantoura, the building of the Palestinian collective memory is built up from the memories of other villages such as Ain Ghazal, Zummarin, Qisarya, Saffurya, Balad al-Sheikh, al-Zeeb, Samakh, Saasaa, Lid, Ramla, and many others, as recounted by the characters belonging to these villages. Radwa Ashour has to a great extent reconstructed the "social morphology" of Palestine in the 1930s (population, forms of assembly and housing, the forms of Palestinian villages and towns, the communication between them including the means of transportation), the Nakba, and the dispersion of Palestinians into the refugee camps of Lebanon and other neighboring countries.

The traditions of marriage celebrations, memorized by the thirteen-year-old Ruqayya in Tantoura, are revived in 1957 at Ain al-Helwa camp in Sidon (Lebanon) during the marriage of Ezz (Amin's brother and Ruqayya's cousin) to a girl from Saffurya. They are also recalled in the marriage of Ruqayya's son Hassan in Piraeus (Greece) to Fatma, who comes from the Palestinian city of Lid. Women chanted the traditional wedding songs:

> *Say to his mother, rejoice and be glad,*
> *Place myrtle on the pillows and henna on our hands.*
> *The wedding is here and the couple is smiling,*
> *The home is my home and the rooms are all mine,*
> *We are engaged, let my enemy die!* (Ashour 2014:4)

The novel continues to delve deeper into memory and bring it to life by setting it in a framework of the Palestinians and their pain. Ruqayya expresses this pain when she promises her son Hassan to continue writing her testimony: "I'll try, Hassan. But what if I die? The writing will kill me." Hassan replies:

> *It won't kill you. You're stronger than you think. Memory does not kill. It inflicts unbearable pain, perhaps; but we bear it, and memory changes from a whirlpool that pulls us to the bottom, to a sea we can swim in. We cover distances, we control it, and we dictate to it.* (Ashour 2014:186)

Thus, the value and importance of her testimony go beyond what written history and documents present. It deals with issues beyond those written in official history, issues that are the life and pulse of her people. The documentary value of Ruqayya's testimony lies in its credibility. It vividly expressed the suffering of the refugees, especially the women, in the camps. At the camp are

> *children, girls, women of my own age, elderly women, each of them with the key of her house hung on a cord around her neck, like my mother. In Shatila I learned that the world of women is more compassionate than the world of men. The men were formed into factions, each with its office and territory and armed young men. They differed and quarreled like cocks. Oh my God, cocks with weapons! And cocks at home, too; they came back to their women and issued orders and prohibitions. The woman is plunged into her daily chores: She picks through the lentils and the rice. She makes mujaddara lentils for seven or ten or fifteen people.* (Ashour 2014:117)

The Memory of Women's Struggle

Ruqayya has never given much thought to her life. Her biography is thus considered an intimate and true testimony about the lives of many Palestinian women whose days are a struggle for survival despite the difficulties. It is a struggle to preserve culture and memory against all forms of threats, and to raise children and instill the spirit of resistance in them.

Besides being a lively and true testimony of the Palestinian memory, Ruqayya's story reveals in depth the lives of asylum-seekers and refugees, especially women. It reveals the minute, lively details of this life which are difficult for the official history to document and record. Ruqayya says, for example, "I suddenly sit up in bed, after lying there between sleep and waking. I count on my fingers: our house in Tantoura; my uncle Abu Amin's old house in Sidon; the marital home, in Sidon also; the house on the Tariq al-Jadida in Beirut; then Abu Dhabi, then Alexandria. The seventh will be there in Sidon, at the gate" (Ashour 2014:338–339). These are not the kinds of details that find their way into official archives.

The struggle not to forget the story—the story of the loss of homeland and the displacement of its people, the story of the massacres Israel committed against them, and the story of asylum—has hope as its ultimate goal. Accordingly, the story is passed from the parents to the children, then to the grandchildren. Ruqayya's daughter, Maryam, complains about the lesson her mother keeps repeating: "Your father was ... your grandfather Abu Sadiq was ... your maternal uncles ... your grandfather Abu Amin was ... ," and the refrain: 'We're Palestinians. Refugees. Children of the camps'" (Ashour 2014:231). In the shelter during the time of the Israeli invasion of Lebanon, Ruqayya "would talk and talk about one subject, never deviating from it: Tantoura. She would talk about it continuously and in detail, attracting the attention of those who heard her. She always ended with the same words: 'When we go back home, I beg you to come and visit us. The village is beautiful, it's worthy of you, and you are worthy of it'" (Ashour 2014:168–169).

The novel *al-Tanturiya* appears to be a two-level oral testimony. The first is internal, where women play a primary role in preserving the memory of the Palestinian people and their cause, relying mainly on the oral heritage; the second is an external level that uses the narrative of the novel to present the collective Palestinian consciousness of historical continuity as well as the unspoken in the lives of women. An article entitled *Horoub al-Thakira* (The Wars of Memory) claims that some Jewish new historians have started to "disclose what is silenced in the curriculum and history books, and that one of them has discovered the unknown 1948 Tantoura massacre. Finkelstein[1] sums up the argument by saying that the tears shed by those acting as victims are not, in fact,

---

1 Norman Finkelstein is an anti-Zionist Jewish historian.

real; they are rather crocodile tears."[2] In this sense, haven't *al-Tanturiya* and its women participated in the wars of memory, especially at the cognitive level?

Tchari: **Unregistered Diaries**

In *Tchari* (Kajji 2013), the focus is on the tragedy of the Iraqis after three wars: Gulf War I, Gulf War II and the subsequent American invasion and occupation of Iraq, and the struggle against al-Qa'ida and other armed Islamist organizations in the country. *Tchari* tells the story of an Iraqi Christian family whose members are scattered throughout the world. The story of this family is similar to that of thousands of Iraqis, especially Christians, who have been forcibly expelled from their homeland.

In the context of this Iraqi tragedy, the testimonies of three women are built and intersect. The novelist, from her Parisian exile, writes a story entitled *Tchari* whose chapters are dominated by nostalgia for Iraq and its war-stricken people, in order to preserve the country's oral history. She also "writes poetry about the dear ones who have been separated and can no longer be reunited except on the atlas map" (Kajji 2013:151–152). She explains to her son, Alexander, the meaning of the word *tchari* in classical Arabic: *"tafarraqu aydi Saba'"* (the dispersion of the Sabaeans)[3] (2013:90).

The narrator resorts to writing and poetry to heal the wounds of separation, displacement, and alienation. She narrates from Paris the story of her childhood home through the story of her aunt, Dr. Wardia Alexander, who is in her eighties. During the course of half a century, her aunt healed thousands of women, then became the first Iraqi refugee in France after the European and American countries opened their doors to Iraqi refugees, especially Christians. Dr. Wardia's three sons had previously been scattered to three different countries. Dr. Wardia

---

2 Khairy Mansur, "Horoub al-thakira," *al-Khaleej*, May 5, 2013. http://articles.islamweb.net/media/index.php?page=article&lang=A&id=186523
3 Saba' is a tribe that lived in east Yemen and became a kingdom in the 10th century BC. It is known for its queen, Sheba, and Marib Dam. When the dam was destroyed the kingdom collapsed and the Sabaeans were scattered in all directions. The expression is an Arabic proverb referring to the dispersion of a people.

came to this country knowing nothing about its people. . . . Whoever sees her pushing her wheelchair . . . cannot believe that these two palms with the blue veins engraved on them are the same magic hands whose trained fingers toured the secret caves of women to untie, scrape, clean, refine, heal and bring happy tidings. (Kajji 2013:18–19)

The doctor's story is the story of a pioneering woman who studies medicine in the 1940s. She is among 13 female students, only eight of whom finished their studies; "they loved medicine and served patients till retirement and death without neglect" (Kajji 2013:79).

She opens the first obstetrics practice in the rural town of Diwaniyah, where she is appointed as a doctor in 1955—a thin, single young woman planning to work for a year in this town six hours away by train from her family in Baghdad. Dr. Wardia ends up living there for more than half a century. She marries Dr. Gergis Mansour and gives birth before moving with her family to Baghdad, where her husband falls ill. She, her sisters, and another doctor are the first women to drive a car in the streets of Diwaniyah: "Every girl in the Alexander family held her car keys after her graduation from university" (Kajji 2013:126).

The Iraqi Memory

What will concern us in this context is the extent to which the history of this Iraqi Christian family coincides with the social history of Iraq, especially that relating to the social fabric which the official history ignores. The beauty of this fabric springs from its diversity, in which patriotic ties are more important than those of sects, creeds, and ethnicities.

Dr. Wardia's father, Alexander, was born in Mosul during the Ottoman Empire. The family moves to Baghdad when Wardia is five, so that her brother Solomon can pursue his passion for the study of the Arabic language. He had been the top student in Arabic in Mosul, which is how the Qur'an came into their house: the custom is to give it as a prize for the top student in the language of the Qur'an (Kajji 2013:64). Solomon becomes an army officer and takes part in the June War. Wardia's husband, Dr. Gergis, serves in the first Palestinian war, which makes him a staunch Nasserite, "and he fell sick and died while dreaming of liberation" (Kajji 2013:108).

Wardia narrates that, at Diwaniyah, though "she was a believer in Jesus and the intercession of Mary, she attended the Qur'anic recitals at al-Husayn at the time of Ashura'.... When she moved to Baghdad, she continued visiting the mawalid held by Um Muhammad—her neighbor on 52nd Street" (Kajji 2013:171). A photo of her son, Buraq, as a child, walking in the Ashura' procession in Diwaniyah, is kept by his sister in Toronto. He

> *was walking with the rhythm of the sounds and the beats on the chest while women were standing and pointing their hands to the sidewalk. ... Look! Look! ... A boy with long blond hair with a golden cross hanging from his neck is walking along with those who slash their torsos and those who cut their heads with swords till they bleed in the convoy of al-Husseini.* (Kajji 2013:186)

Cross-Testimonies of Women

The rhythm of the narrative flow is that of a narrator who forcibly lives alienated from a country she loves. Her alienation is parallel to that of her aunt (Dr. Wardia) in France and Henda (Dr. Wardia's daughter) in Canada. It is homesickness for a country that was once beautiful despite all its flaws such as poverty, corruption, ignorance, obsolete beliefs, honor crimes, and patriarchy. In comparison to the dark present, the past remains beautiful. Each time she checks an Iraqi news website, the narrator's feelings are the same:

> *It seems to me that I see pictures of children who died as a result of malnutrition, polluted water and radioactive weapons. ... All of them thrown at the chests of their mothers who died either at a suicide bombing in the Doura District, a massacre at Fallujah, or drowning under A'imah Bridge or at Sayedet al-Najat Church.* (Kajji 2013:239–240)

The narrator recounts scenes and stories as if she is repairing the threads of the Iraqi social fabric that was torn apart and split up by wars. Gatherings of

> *relatives only occur during funerals. Picnics are not safe. The areas are divided, and visits can cause worry. Even attending sermons in church could end in a tragedy. There are no clubs, dabka parties, new*

year's celebrations, Way of the Cross rituals, Lady's Day, or Khedr Ilias Day. (Kajji 2013:131–132)

Eventually, Dr. Wardia's family receives a frightening message: "Peace be upon those who follow the right path. You have 10 days from today to implement this fatwa and give us your daughter as the lawful wife of the Amir [prince] of our community, or we shall kill you all, take your home, ye infidels, and to hell you will all go" (Kajji 2013:129). Dr. Wardia, whose "clinic was her world," has been "worn down by her years of life now that she is retired from the hospital; she pulled her swollen leg to the old Toyota car to start the engine. Her car takes her to the clinic. Because the car has so often gone back and forth on this road, it has memorized the holes, the bumps, and the faces of the police officers" (Kajji 2013:19–20). Dr. Wardia's daughter, Yasmine, marries quickly and moves to Dubai to escape from a bad situation that will only become worse.

Iraq in the Memory of Its Women

Tchari and *al-Tanturiya* are similar, though their themes and artistic construction are different. Both are trying to build a collective memory from the memories of women and the course of their lives. But *Tchari* neglects Iraq's official history of regimes, governance, and the like to focus on the popular social fabric, female memory, and female history. Like Ruqayya from Tantoura, who learns that the world of women is more merciful than that of men when she sees the Palestinian camp split into factions and the men fighting like chickens, Dr. Wardia remembers that

> *their national day was on the same day as the French and the memory of the march towards the Bastille prison. A republic here and a republic there! It is as if the free officers wanted to emulate this famous date on purpose, but their dreams went astray. They passed by quickly; they were similar only in cruelty, and different in results.* (Kajji 2013:105)

Tchari historicizes the Iraqi social fabric by remembering Dr. Wardia eating *kebbah* in Mosul, sharing the happiness and the sadness of her neighbors, enjoying the warmth of ordinary communication, which entails kindness, generosity, and love.

When a woman delivers her baby in peace and it is a boy, she must attend all the banquets held for him. They send a car to her house to take her and her daughter, Yasmine, to the banquet. They welcome her and offer her cold water, Pepsi, and baklava as if she is Queen Elizabeth of England. The car takes her back home, and they offer her boxes filled with dates, loaves of furnace bread, and Syrian amber. (Kajji 2013:23)

Tchari and *al-Tanturiya* both rely on elements of oral heritage, as is evident in the narrative memories. Unlike *al-Tanturiya*, *Tchari* does not deconstruct the one collective memory into separate memories. Instead, *Tchari* builds one collective memory to represent the original beautiful time, when peaceful coexistence and human relations connected different social groups together; it is an original memory which contradicts a more recent memory, a memory in which the narrator is a stranger to the Iraqi social body. It is a memory that the current time imposes on the Iraqis, including women: "Women's clothes have changed, and the veil is now covering all heads, competing with the traditional *'abaya*" (Kajji 2013:21).

The narrator's testimony makes Henda—the young doctor—and her struggle a modern version of her mother, reacting to the forced memory now being formed. It also emphasizes the role of the Iraqi woman in resistance and change. Henda, who migrated to Canada, works at a hospital in Manitoba with other immigrant Iraqis, on an Indian reservation that lies in the lakes region in the middle of Canada. It is far from where she lives in Toronto, and it takes her long hours by plane, then by car, to reach her husband and children. Every Monday morning, she travels to the hospital by plane with her baby, then they return together to Toronto on Friday evening. The entire trip takes "less than seven hours. This is much easier than the Jaljala Road between Baghdad and Amman during the days of the siege" (Kajji 2013:211).

In a letter to her mother, Henda asks her: "Didn't you go to work upon graduation in the villages and the countryside? Today, I follow your steps but in a different place. Diwaniyah is better than Manitoba" (Kajji 2013:211). Henda refuses to sell any of her belongings in Baghdad because she does not want to deprive her children "of a foothold in a country which will remain their homeland, no matter how far east or west they go" (Kajji 2013:196).

Conclusion

This research attempts to show the social function of remembrance, especially for women. It is based on the fact that the self is the sum of what we remember, and that we cannot only recall memories or live them. Instead, and more importantly, we reconstruct them. However, this process faces several obstacles, the most important of which is forgetfulness.

In the light of this discussion, we have shown the means through which the female memory can be extracted and saved from forgetfulness and loss. Culture is not only "a way of thinking and life," but it is also "a memory," "an identity," and "a place." The two novels are important for their "narrative identity," which fills in the gaps of the collective awareness of the historical continuity of those women who are ignored by the official history even if their names are engraved in places: "Here was the clinic of Dr. Wardia Alexander." "Women point to this wrecked building while passing in front of it on their way home in al-Ghadeer, Tal Muhammad, Camp Sara, Zeyouna, and New Baghdad. New Baghdad had been one of the best districts in the capital before its markets turned into dunghills and brackish water" (Kajji 2013:248).

In *Tchari*, Henda says that "the home is not just a matter of walls, ceiling, garden and roof, but it is a meaning which embodies various meanings inside it" (Kajji 2013:197). In the same vein, we may add that homelands are large homes that embrace their citizens while disregarding their differences. They do not refer to places only, but also belonging, identity, history, and memory. Women have played a key role in recalling the narrative or oral history in the process of a resisting memory. This role is evident in the centrality of the female narrators as well as the expansive space in which the lives of the female characters emerged in the novels.

References

Ansart, Pierre. 1974. *Les idéologies politiques*. Paris: PUF.
Amir, Yusri. 1993. "Interview with Elias Khoury," *Majallat al-Adaab*, 87 (July/August).
Ashour, Radwa. 2014. *The Woman from Tantoura*. Kay Heikkinen, trans. Cairo: American University in Cairo Press.
Halbwachs, Maurice. 1997. *La mémoire collective*. Paris: Albin Michel.

References

———. 2012. *Les Cadres sociaux de la mémoire* (version numérique par Jean-Marie Tremblay). Chicoutimi: Université du Québec.
Kajji, In'am. 2013. *Tchari*. Beirut: Dar al-Gadid.
Ricoeur, Paul. 1999. *Al-wogoud wal-zaman wal-sard: Falsafat Paul Ricoeur*. Said al-Ghanemi, trans. Beirut: Al-Markaz al-thaqafi al-Arabi.
———. 2000. *La mémoire, l'histoire, l'oubli*. Paris: Éditions du Seuil.
Al-Salibi, Kamal. 2009. *Qira'at fi tholathiyat Gaber Rabie' Beirut madinat al-'alam*. Beirut: Dar Nablus.
Shahayid, Gamal. 2011. *Al-Thakira fil-rowaya al-'arabiya al-mo'asara*. Beirut: Al-Moa'ssasa al-'Arabiya li-l-Dirasat wa-l-Nashr.

CHAPTER 7

Palestinian Memory in Light of New Technology: Opportunities and Challenges

Nahawand El Kaderi Issa

Introduction

This chapter seeks to explore how a nation's people that were banished by force from their land, displaced across the globe, and stripped of their rights are located in the virtual space, in an attempt to examine the opportunities available for young generations to narrate their own experiences and suffering, and to once more take the initiative and document their grandparents' experiences and suffering as well. It is then possible to determine the nature of the challenges these young generations face–especially in terms of raising interest in the cause, as well as the divisions and internal discord that have been growing recently–based on factors that control the memory's selectivity and set its priorities. This has become especially important since current advances in technology and communication have led to freeing the space for expression, helped citizen journalism and the citizen historian to emerge, and created alternative spaces that everyone uses. The use of communications spaces in this way has turned them into multiple, political, electronic spaces that are subject to all kinds of violations. Soon enough, the political expressions of ordinary people started to reveal verbal violence, intolerance, racism, and bigotry. Media forums became, on the one hand, fertile ground for many deviations and spontaneous formulations in the name of the "I," as in "I believe that," and also a kind of outlet for personal and prior judgments, as a result of their inability to produce quality debates. On the other hand, these forums became spaces that witness reactions to events, assertion of individual opinion, and confrontation with the

Introduction

Other, spaces which include many validated opinions. In this regard, it can be said that these forums feed the civic culture and contribute to expanding the general space.

This virtual world, full of accelerated and conflicting waves, visited by some users who are demanding and selective and by others who are easily distracted and prone to drown in the clamor of too much information, is juxtaposed with a realistic world that witnesses continuous jolts, transformations, and severe conflicts that emerge in the form of various types of information warfare, where it is difficult to distinguish between producer and consumer, inquirer and informant, narrator and listener, viewer and viewed. This is accompanied by a glorification of instantaneousness and immediacy, while hysterically spiraling toward the urgent and the rapid, making the media seem suspended between two voids: the despicable, unrecognized past and the worrying, unthought-of future.

In light of this reality in the Arab world, which novelist Ibrahim Nasrallah described as "flaccid and now completely degenerated, remembrance becomes a major issue, and war becomes the war of memory. This war on Palestinian memory is launched on two levels: the enemy and its media allies, and a conspiring Arab media that has now become a guardian for the Zionist narrative, especially on satellite television channels."[1] Or perhaps the war is oblivious to what goes on around it, content to merely use mechanisms and contexts that it did not take part in shaping.

In conjunction with these transformations surrounded by paradoxes that are enhanced by major illusions, we see groups and individuals who have suffered from marginalization as a result of the selectivity of historical narratives and media messages, and who are trying to contradict this logic and to narrate their own experiences themselves with no mediator. Thus, websites were founded by minorities, the oppressed, the vulnerable, and the marginalized. These websites aim on the one hand to document experiences, whether individual or collective, and on the other hand to maintain the collective memory, as a means of preserving identity.

We can find on the internet many websites, blogs, and social media pages that vary in their purposes, aims, and content. These are sites

---

1 Zaman al-Okaili, "Ibrahim Nasrallah: al-hakaya allati la naktubuha tusbih milkan li a'da'ina," *al-Safir*, June 30, 2015.

where the individual and the collective, the Palestinian cause and personal issues, and past, present, and future are all articulated. They are also sites where the interests of their owners, the nature of their work, their gender, their place of residence, the language they use, and the audience they target all vary. In spite of this broad space which brings together all groups, all ages and trends, and in spite of the internet operators who impose their own indirect terms and conditions on users, it is clear from the outset that talks on the Palestinian cause are no longer confined to their traditional frame. Now that the history of this cause has been subjected to selective and unilateral perspectives that are often taken out of their social implications, and out of local, regional, and international contexts, all talk on the cause has become incongruously scattered. Collective memory has become more prone to fragmentation because of a number of factors. Chief among them are:

- The selectivity of individual memory, once it became free from group pressure.
- The selectivity of internet operators over the selectivity of individual memory.
- The disappearance of this cause in the labyrinths of political conflicts on all levels.
- The fragility of collective memories and their relation to historical time and the chronicling of the past with terms, expressions, and images of the present, or dealing with the present with the memory, imagination, and projections of the past.

It is important to note that researching this case brings with it complications and obstacles that put the researcher in a state of constant worry if the goal is to move from merely describing it to actually thinking about it and what it means, especially in light of the interaction between memory and historical research. In this context, Wajih Kawtharani wonders "whether historical research and the historian's profession could have a corrective role for memories that lean towards the mythical in light of the attraction between the past and the present and in the midst of the conflict between collective historical memories that have not yet settled and are constantly stirred by questions of the present and its local worries" (Kawtharani 2000:24–25).

Websites

Although many other issues have arisen for Palestinians in recent years, their preoccupation with their memory as their lost place is noteworthy.[2] Some believe that this memory "does not establish anything as much as it asserts its presence, and this in a way seems consistent with the daily use of memory, which in turn changes the subject matter of memory as a place. Photographs that the Palestinian museum has been collecting and digitizing for months, and gathering testimonies from their owners in a project called 'Family Album,' are not seen merely as archive photographs, but as places of residence."[3]

Within this conception of memory, many websites devoted to Palestinian oral history emerged, with diverse aims and administrators. For example, there were institutions working on archiving this history scientifically, such as the "Palestinian Oral History Archive" project, while others race against time to publish the largest number of interviews before all members of the Nakba generation pass away. Some are family efforts while others are the efforts of researchers and individuals, even including one Israeli anti-occupation institution that attempted to historicize the Nakba in its own way. There is also some diversity in the interests of Palestinian websites, which points to a societal awareness of history in their founders as they adopt mechanisms that link individual experiences to their social contexts and make the past part of the present. Thus, these websites range from the public to the private, and from the all-encompassing to the specific, linking issues of gender, education, and politics, as well as matters related to daily life, to the mother cause. They also provide answers to the problem of the connection between memory and history, between the individual and collective consciousnesses, which historians who rely on oral history as a primary source of information on social and political life still find.

Some of these websites are:

- The "Palestinian Oral History Archive," now under construction, is the product of several institutions. These include the Jana Foundation, the Nakba Archive, the Issam Fares Institute for Public Policy

---

2 Research assistant Taghrid al-Samiri collected all data in this study.
3 "Album al-'a'ila al-falastiniyya: al-suwar bewasfiha makanan," *al-Modon*, May 25, 2015.

and International Affairs, and the American University of Beirut library. The oral archive contains 800 interviews, which is about 1,000 hours of recordings, with individuals who lived through the 1948 Nakba and lived in Palestinian refugee camps in Lebanon. These people tell stories of Palestine before 1948, the experience of displacement, and the establishment of camps. The archive also includes the experience of women in Ain al-Hilweh camp during the 1982 Israeli invasion and what followed, in addition to Palestinian folk tales and songs.

- The "Palestine Remembered" website, http://www.palestineremembered.com, is a non-profit project founded in 2000 to serve Palestinians. It is now one of the biggest and most important Palestinian websites. The main motive for establishing this website, according to its administrators, is to "preserve Palestinian memory from loss and tampering." In 2003, the website embarked on a project on the Nakba's oral history. So far, more than 600 interviews, consisting of over 3,000 hours of recording, have been conducted with people who lived through the 1948 Nakba in Palestinian towns and cities.

- iNakba is an Israeli project in the form of a smart phone application that transports users to pre-displacement Palestine (copied from al-Jazeera.net). It was created to accomplish the difficult task of identifying the names of Nakba villages that existed before 1948. The free application provides a map of Palestine covered with hundreds of brown dots, each dot marking an Arab village that was wiped out in 1948. The app was developed by Zochrot ('remembering' in Hebrew), an Israeli anti-occupation NGO founded in 2005 with both Arab and Jewish members. According to its website, the organization's aim is "raising the Nakba to the awareness of the broad Jewish public." Zochrot believes that knowledge of the Nakba is a necessary condition for the Jews to acknowledge responsibility for their part in the Palestinian Nakba, which in turn is a major condition for future reconciliation with Palestinians. The application provides a complete description of each village: its population before 1948, the date of its occupation, its history, the settlements built on its remnants, and a photograph of the village itself or one of its houses before that year. The application, available for OS and

Android devices, draws its information from the book *So That We Do Not Forget: Palestinian Villages Destroyed by Israel in 1948 and Names of Their Martyrs*, by Walid al-Khalidi, published by the Institute for Palestine Studies in 1997 (my translation). Information is provided in three languages: Arabic, English, and Hebrew.[4]

- The website http://refugee.ps is dedicated to the "We Will Return" project, which calls for the refugees' right to return. The project is organized by AlTawasol Forum Society. The oral documentation unit for refugees was formed in 2011 as part of the Refugee Rights Program, to document the oral history of the Palestinian Nakba. The project focuses on recording and preserving all information on Palestine before and after the Nakba. The unit's observations focus on traditions and customs; folklore; accent or dialect; the chronological order of events before and after the Nakba; and the description of Palestinian refugees during their displacement from their villages, cities, and countries. The latter includes the paths chosen by refugees during their migration (means of transportation, the suffering they endured, the water places they visited while migrating, the camps they temporarily stayed at before finally living in exile). The unit's observations also include descriptions of the suffering of refugees in permanent camps in exile (schools, housing, water, electricity, workers' training center, workplaces), how refugees felt while visiting their land and property from which they were expelled or while viewing photographs of villages and towns from which they were expelled and which are found on the Palestine Remembered website, and their opinions about returning to their houses, fields, and workplaces. Oral history is available on the website in both visual and written formats.
- The Women for Palestine website (www.womenfpal.com) describes itself as follows: "Women of Palestine is a feminist media organization that works in Gaza Strip and focuses on raising awareness of

---

4 On its website, Zochrot states that the application includes maps with the features of all the Palestinian towns that were torn down after they had been occupied, all the towns that were partially demolished, and even those that remained as they were but whose residents were kicked out. According to the organization, the application also includes historical information, footage, and photographs of these towns. The application is interactive and users can upload pictures of demolished towns, share them, and follow updates on selected towns.

the Palestinian cause, particularly the struggle of Palestinian women, and on showing how these women persevere and struggle."
- The official website of the al-Ramahi family (www.al-ramahi-diwan). This website is a personal family project carried out by the al-Ramahi family. They recorded the narratives of the family's elders and posted them on a website for the family. These stories, an oral narration of the Nakba's history, introduce the family's younger generations to the history of their ancestors.
- The Aswat Group (www.aswatgroup.org) is a Palestinian website for a group of lesbian and transgender, liberal, Palestinian women. The website lists its goals as follows:

    o   To provide spaces for support and self-fulfillment for LBTQI women
    o   To change, critique, and deconstruct the dominant male discourse and turn it into a politically, socially, sexually, economically, and gender-wise fair discourse
    o   To raise awareness of and provide knowledge about lesbianism, gender, and sexual pluralism for educational staff and service providers

- The website www.mahmoud.dk is an individual experiment carried out by Palestinian researcher Mahmoud Youssef Eissa, a coordinator for a project on old Palestinian history and heritage at the University of Copenhagen's Faculty of Theology in Denmark. Eissa created this website to broadcast interviews on oral Palestinian history along with a Danish translation.

Blogs

Perhaps the selectivity of memory and the means to extract and document memories become more complicated when research adopts a gender-based approach. We notice an interest on the part of some blogs in showcasing compound gender-based violence against Palestinian women, especially female prisoners in Israeli occupation prisons. Female prisoners in these prisons, who already endure brutal torture, cannot escape the terrifying, questioning gazes of their society, which wonders what happened to them inside the occupation prisons. For example, women's issues occupy center stage in more than one way on the blog of Palestinian journalist Hedaya Shamun. On her blog, Shamun has published articles and studies on Palestinian women's reality, including "Palestinian Women Journalists and Societal Challenges," "Palestinian Women in Media," "Domestic Violence," and others. Under the title "Female Prisoners behind Bars," Shamun writes the narratives and testimonies of female Palestinian prisoners in Israeli detention centers and the testimonies of freed prisoners, especially about the domestic and societal violence to which these prisoners are subjected. Shamun quotes one prisoner as saying: "He [her former husband] kicked me and my daughter out when I was released from an Israeli prison. I found myself on the streets. He insulted me because I was at Israeli occupation prisons for over a year, then he married another and cast me aside. He even started punishing me with his cruelty in the mornings and evenings and calling me the most hideous of names." Shamun quotes her further: "Yes, neighbors and relatives scold us. We are met with scary gazes in their eyes as they wonder, 'What happened to you in occupation prisons?' I always answer without them even asking, 'I glorified the name of Palestine. You must be proud of me, not tie me with your eyes to my body.'"

Under the section "Hekayati" ("My Story"), Shamun writes about situations she encountered with women who were victims of violence.

> *She tried in all sorts of ways to convince her husband and he did not hesitate to hit her and to physically and psychologically hurt her. In spite of her family's many attempts to help her, societal customs allow men freedom to deal with their wives however they want to, even if these men are oppressive and domineering. We tried to help her many times, but her fear that he would find out that someone knew of his violence against her and prevent her from pursuing her education was something he had threatened her with before. So she does not try to make matters worse, according to her beliefs. She has a daughter and doesn't want to be called a divorcee or to live away from her daughter and feel heartbroken over her. So she remains silent and accepts the continuing circle of violence.* (http://hedaya.blogspot.com/)

Shamun continues: "Samah is not the only human being who suffers in silence, behind the scenes and closed doors. She is not the only one trying to step out of the cocoon of domestic violence, but she is the only one who realizes that her future and ambition are just around the corner: it is a question of to be or not to be."

On the other hand, Shahd Abu Salama, a Palestinian student from the Gaza Strip who studies at a London university and is the daughter of a prisoner at an Israeli detention center, focuses her blog—which is written in English—on the importance of remembrance, by recalling narratives of grandmothers and their insistence on telling their grandsons and granddaughters stories of their original village before the Nakba and before they migrated to the Gaza Strip. The young woman then connects her grandmother's narrative to later Nakba generations and how they were brought up on bedtime stories about their beautiful green villages. Their grandparents' stories were even in songs sung to them before bed, according to Abu Salama (see @shahdabusalama on Twitter).

Social Networking Pages

To see how the Palestinian cause appears on pages of social network users, I followed eight Facebook pages of Palestinian journalists, ensuring gender equality by having four males and four females. I also made sure that the selected sample, as small as it was, included individuals from different parts of the Palestinian territories. The sample included one male and two female journalists from the Gaza Strip, one female and two male journalists from the West Bank, and one male and one female journalist from Jerusalem. I also tried to select professional journalists known for their criticism of both ruling parties in Palestine (the Hamas administration and the Palestinian National Authority), and who belong to three different age groups (20–30 years, 30–40 years, and 40–50 years). The goal was to learn the topics that male and female journalists discuss and identify posts that turned into public issues. The first one of these was the case of Khader Adnan, an administrative detainee who went on a hunger strike. The second was the photograph of Tarek al-Sadda, who protected an Israeli policewoman from stones hurled at her by Palestinians, while the third was about the arrest of Gaza journalist Mushira al-Hajj. The eight Facebook pages belonged to the following journalists.

From the West Bank. Naela Khalil: A Palestinian journalist from Balata camp in Nablus. Born in 1977, Khalil got her MA in media at a

UK university. She worked at *al-Ayyam*, a Palestinian newspaper. She has received many awards, including the Samir Kassir Award in 2008 for her article "Palestinians Pay the Price of Hatred: Political Arrest as a Means of Settling Accounts between Hamas and Fatah," written in Arabic. Khalil is currently in charge of *al-Arabi al-Jadid* newspaper in Ramallah. She is known for criticizing both Hamas and the Palestinian Authority; she and her family have been subject to the authority's harassment because of her writings and stances.

Walid Batrawi: A Palestinian journalist working in the field since 1991. He currently works for BBC Palestine as project manager for BBC media action. He is also a trainer in investigative journalism. Batrawi worked as a correspondent for *Al-Jazeera English* and BBC Radio. He was awarded the Lorenzo Natali Media Prize from the European Union for his coverage of human rights and democracy in the Middle East.

Fady Abu Seada: A Palestinian journalist from Bethlehem and correspondent for *al-Quds al-Arabi*.

From Gaza. Samia al-Zubaidi: A Palestinian journalist from Gebalya in Gaza. She has worked for a number of media outlets. She is an activist, a journalism trainer, and a member of several unions and NGOs.

Moustafa Ibrahim: A Palestinian journalist, researcher, and rights activist at the Independent Commission for Human Rights in Gaza.

Mushira Tawfik: A Palestinian journalist from Khan Yunis in Gaza. She works as an independent journalist for a number of institutions, including Hadf News.

From Jerusalem. Ahmed al-Bedeiri: A Palestinian journalist who was a correspondent for the BBC, then for Paltoday. He is currently a news producer for ABC News.

Christine Renawi: Correspondent for the official channel of Palestine in Jerusalem.

The Israeli occupation and its continuous violations against the Palestinian people made up the largest percentage of topics discussed on the Facebook pages, followed by living conditions, then criticisms of social behavior and practices. These were followed by media issues, prisoners' affairs, criticism of Hamas, and gender issues. At the bottom of the list were resistance, rights, and freedoms, and criticism of some Palestinian factions and parties.

For example, Walid Batrawi criticizes the habit of sounding sirens and honking car horns that accompany weddings, wondering: How can two newlyweds start their lives with this amount of chaos, recklessness, and violence? Naela Khalil condemns parents who buy their children deadly toys that harm others. She also harshly criticizes an advertisement for Jawwal communications company that says: "Jawwal makes your wait at barriers more fun," saying, "How shameful of them." Ahmed Bedeiri condemns the habit of lighting fireworks when children pass at school, saying that it only irritates others and is a waste of money.

Concerning gender differences, it was noted that females' priorities were discussing topics related to the Israeli occupation's violation of Palestinians' rights, followed by prisoners' affairs, criticism of social practices, and gender issues. Next came criticism of Hamas and complaints about living conditions, both of which were given equal importance. These were followed by criticism of the Palestinian Authority, and finally discussions of rights and freedoms. On the other hand, males primarily focused on living conditions, then on the Israeli occupation violations. Next were discussions of media affairs, criticism of social practices, criticism of the Authority, criticism of Hamas, criticism of factions and parties, resistance, and rights and freedoms. At the bottom of these priorities, with a very small percentage, were discussions on gender issues. What is notable is the lack of males' interest in prisoners' affairs.

On the subject of individuals returning to their original place of residence, both male and female journalists in the Gaza Strip first touched upon people's living conditions. For the West Bank journalists, the chief topic for both males and females was criticizing citizens' conduct. Male and female journalists in Jerusalem primarily discussed the crimes committed by Israelis, particularly in Jerusalem. Their discussions ranged from settler crimes to occupation crimes, demolition of houses, and prevention of access to houses using concrete blocks. They also discussed break-ins and trespasses into al-Aqsa Mosque. Jerusalem journalists did not pay particular attention to criticizing the Authority or Hamas or even citizens' conduct.

Social Networking Pages

We will examine in more detail the posts that contributed in one way or another to turning some issues into public ones, in chronological order from the oldest to the newest.

Khader Adnan, the administrative detainee who went on a hunger strike. Naela Khalil dedicated her Facebook page to documenting the details of the case of Khader Adnan, an administrative detainee in the Israeli occupation prisons who went on a hunger strike that lasted 55 days. Khalil posted interviews she conducted with Adnan's wife. After Adnan's health worsened, his wife and children went to the hospital where he was, to support him. On that day, Khalil wrote: "The detainee's wife said: I am now at Sarafand Hospital's yard and I announce my sit-in and declare I am on a hunger strike, and my six children and I will not move from here." Then she posted the wife's request to get in touch with Arab members of the Knesset and all those who are in solidarity with them, to join them at the hospital, which has been located in the occupied territories since 1948. Khalil posted phone numbers of Arab Knesset members, urging Adnan's supporters to call and text them. Khalil was following up on the arrival of supporters moment by moment and documenting their names. Several hours later, there were hundreds of activists in front of the hospital, in addition to Arab Knesset members who participated in last-minute

Tarek al-Sadda, who shielded an Israeli policewoman from Palestinian stones.

negotiations against the backdrop of chants below Adnan's room: "Ours is a human revolution declared by Khader Adnan." A little while later, Khalil wrote that Adnan's family joined him in the room to celebrate his decision to end his hunger strike after the Israeli occupation agreed to his conditions, including a condition to never detain him administratively again.

This photograph spread very quickly on social media on August 2, 2015. It was taken after Israeli settlers burned Ali Dawabsheh, a Palestinian infant, alive. The photograph shows two Palestinians protecting an Israeli policewoman from stones hurled at her between a Palestinian village and a settlers' outpost. The photograph was posted on the Facebook page of an Israeli man who is friends with the photographer with a caption saying:

> *Shaoul (the photographer) and I see many photographs in the West Bank like this beautiful one. It represents a reversal in consciousness. The Jew who belonged to a minority and came to power became an idiot, and the Palestinian became an oppressed individual. When we came back from there, they were looking at us as alien bodies. This is not the Holocaust, and I am not German. The majority of Palestinians are the Jews we once were.*

Naela Khalil tried to follow up on this story and capitalize on it to create a different image of Palestinians. She spoke to one of the two men in the photograph. On August 4, 2015, she wrote:

> *Days ago, Zakariya al-Sadda (on the left) and the head of the Qusra village council (on the right) were covering assaults of settlers on Qusra when clashes and chaos erupted between demonstrators on the one hand and the occupation's army and police on the other. Minutes later, this policewoman realized she was standing among the occupation's police force and started crying out of fear. Palestinians were hurling stones everywhere. At that moment, an occupation soldier was about to start sniping at demonstrators to secure the policewoman's return to his side. Zakariya al-Sadda shouted at the soldier in Hebrew: "Do not shoot at the demonstrators. I will protect her." In this regard, al-Sadda*

says: "I had two choices before me: to see the soldier snipe at a Palestinian and kill him, or to tell him that I will protect the policewoman from stones so that you will not shoot at demonstrators."

Khalil explains the story of the photograph, which many people circulated, saying that she preferred to hear the story from al-Sadda himself, and that according to the video she watched, al-Sadda was filming a video of an attack by settlers on the opposite side and was not taking a selfie as some thought.

Khalil's post clarifying the story was shared many times and was translated into English, which implies that Palestinians, through their interaction with everyday events as citizens, are capable of creating a new image for themselves that is independent of official and partisan media.

The arrest of Gaza journalist Mushira al-Hajj. On August 6, 2015, Samia al-Zubaidi led a battle of a different kind to support one of her fellow journalists who was arrested by the police in Gaza. She wrote:

Journalist Mushira Tawfik al-Hajj is now detained at Ansar Prison as per an order from the general prosecutor in Gaza regarding a post she wrote about medical errors in one of the Gaza Strip hospitals. In her post, she wrote: "Before her mother saw or held her, days after she was placed in an incubator, so-called doctors at al-Aqsa martyrs' morgue caused the death of an infant named Swar, after the umbilical cord was cut before the mother's C-section was complete, and caused a dislocation in her arm during delivery. For what crime was Swar killed, you sons of bitches?"

Al-Hajj originally posted this statement on her Facebook account on April 14, 2015. Afterwards, she followed up on this case with the family and the hospital, which accused her of making up information about the case. Al-Zubaidi called on all journalists to sit in at Ansar Prison until her colleague al-Hajj was released. In the context of al-Zubaidi's thanks to those who responded and supported the right to self-expression, she urged them to prepare for escalations to back anyone persecuted for their opinions.

The Tamer Institute

In a remarkable step to institutionalize memory and protect it against disruptions, the Tamer Institute (a non-profit Palestinian institute) trained a team of young men and women to write Palestine's oral history in a literary manner. The institute then posted these texts on social media websites. Topics generally focus on the observations of writers on trips organized by the institute in Palestinian areas. The texts are a collection of literary reflections on their trip. According to the project's managers, the project aims to "deepen the youth's knowledge of the nation." It should be noted that the Tamer Institute has also arranged tours for youths in Jerusalem and meetings with the city's residents; it later documented all the resilience stories they collected in a book published by the institute.

Conclusions

Palestinians see oral history as an act of democracy through which they chronicle their lived experiences and their suffering. They also view it as an effective means of discovering, correcting, and resuscitating their historical memory. Information technology helps them produce a complex culture that brings together individual and collective memories, the past and the present, confrontation of the occupation and self-confrontation, by criticizing social practices, the different facets of political corruption, and power struggles. Due to the ease of communication offered by social media, these people, as individuals or in groups, men and women, managed to overcome hurdles and distances and go beyond political conflicts and narrow interests. They have gathered up their scattered memories and added new meanings to their cause.

Yet excessive optimism about the freedom and the evasion of restrictions and censorship that the internet affords to individuals is refuted by reality for many reasons.

- The digital identity, designed to become a continuous record of activities, now requires users to conform to the requirements of the internet, to interact with its format, to constantly fuel it with new information, and to generalize the personal. This leads to risks that require many forms of censorship, in the form of a degree of control over both the self and others. Self-presentation is

Conclusions

necessarily subjected to a strategy that shapes the desired identity to be revealed in addition to controlling the field of vision (Cadron 2010:321).
- Posting personal pictures and displaying momentary feelings are not public expressions. They do not reflect citizen participation nor do they represent the wisdom of the masses. They are merely social, regular, playful, daily practices on a micro level (Kaplan 2010:161).
- Major players on the internet call for participation by making available various forms of cooperation. They do this in order to make money, not to create a world where people collaborate. Therefore, the spontaneous groupings that spring up on the web are merely a kind of conglomeration based first and foremost on individuality and the individuality of connecting to others. In Web 2.0, any groups that are formed probably stem from spontaneous groupings that can later be restricted or stopped, without the need for prior intention (Kaplan 2010:162).
- Making the relational web exceptionally productive has created a set of particular problems. The first of them is that the standard participatory model based on continuous publication may marginalize other intellectual trends that are less participatory. The second is that the apparent wisdom of the masses, which certain actors may attempt to leverage into a type of power, may implicitly deny the wisdom of experts, mediators, and men of science, and the idea that goes unexpressed online may be stifled under the pressure of the masses or of those who do not speak their language. The third and last problem is that one possible effect of the exchange that occurs before innovation is the exclusion of long-term thinking and indulging in dreams (Kaplan 2010:166).

It is clear from this analysis that Palestinians who seek to document their oral history face complex challenges. It is true that the individual's capacity to escape society's preset identities has grown with the advent of the internet. It is also true that the marginalized and the vulnerable have become more liberal. These are all positive points that could rush us into building hopes and dreams on them. Yet the system that provided these abilities also presents the possibility of molding them in favor of the operators. From this standpoint, these groups need to work on:

- Exerting massive efforts to formulate private issues and turn them into public ones, and to formulate public issues to make them more practical and easier to act upon.
- Applying the electronic archive rules professionally in selection and evaluation, especially since the technological and economic changes that occurred toward the end of the twentieth century resulted in a qualitative deterioration of paper documents. As a result of the diversity in the oral material forms, archiving had to include strict rules for selection and evaluation.[5] As Omnia Amer points out, archivists need to be more than objective keepers of documents. They must come out of the loop of paper and electronic documents to take part in producing documents that form an integral part of their academic and professional work.
- Researchers and academics must examine archived documents, formulate them, and combine analytical approaches in order to produce new concepts and meanings that suit the requirements of the current phase. Artists, scriptwriters, and directors must also work on conveying to the people the meanings of these documents.
- A number of factors must be taken into consideration in all of these endeavors. The first of these is that relaying memories to external data banks may not only threaten the complexity and individuality of the self but also the richness of the culture we share (Rognetta, Jammot, and Tardy 2012:90). The second is that the systems themselves dictate certain rules of conduct and patterns of usage. Very few players dare to breach them. Every new discussion setting acquires work methods that users quickly adjust to. These criteria undeniably produce forms of exclusion that in turn will create new forms of and spaces for discussion, continuously renewing the classical ideal. In discussing the logic that structures the supply and demand of information, one researcher pointed to a logic stemming from daily non-work exchanges between individuals, exchanges that lie on the borders of private space and which in the public sphere create capabilities, media, and collaboration. This is what supports the plurality of reports based on lived individual and emotional experiences (Miège 2010:89). The third is the importance of taking into consideration the influence of the prevailing culture and public ideology in shaping the consciousness and

---

5 Omnia Amer, "A History Disregarded by History," journal.cybrariens.info.

memory of the individual (whether speaker or listener). This is because they affect the conflict of interest and privacy of anyone offering their testimony to history and the receivers of this testimony as well.[6] This is especially true as we are now witnessing a relative democratization of discussions on topics that were for long limited to politicians and experts; access to public discourse is becoming easier, as users' devices allow them to steadily expand their potential for intervention. Merging the new social players, including women, has coincided with a transformation or adaptation for means of exchange, and the current means are no longer compatible with classic rhetoric criteria. The contemporary public space is no longer reserved only for enlightened and institutionalized players, but also includes civil society organizations and the sum total of mass and non-mass media.

To conclude, we find shallowness of attention and scarcity in listening, in contrast to the abundance of narratives and narrators. This calls for continuous, attentive work in more than one area and on various fronts, in parallel between the real and the virtual worlds, and between the worlds of those who produce, code, and send, and those who receive, interpret, and decode.

References

Cadron, D. 2010. "Confiner le clair-obscur: Réflexions sur la protection de la vie personnelle sur le Web 2.0." In F. Millerand, S. Proulx, and J. Rueff, eds. *Web social: Mutation de la communication*, 316–328. Quebec: Presses de l'Université du Québec.

Kaplan, D. 2010. "Vouloir un web coopératif." In F. Millerand, S. Proulx, and J. Rueff, eds. *Web social: Mutation de la communication*, 160–167. Quebec: Presses de l'Université du Québec.

Kawtharani, W. 2000. *al-Dhakirah wa-l-tarikh fi al-qarn al-'ashreen al-taweel*. Beirut: Dar al-Tali'a.

Miège, B. 2010. *L'espace public contemporain*. Paris: PUG (Presse Universitaire de Grenoble).

Rognetta, J., J. Jammot, and F. Tardy. 2010. *La république des réseaux: Périls et promesses de la révolution numérique*. Paris: Fayard.

---

6 Amer, "A History Disregarded by History."

III

Ethical and Methodological Questions

CHAPTER 8

Documenting the Oral History of Iraqis in Times of Conflict: Challenges, Ethics, and Standards of Practice

Lucine Taminian

This chapter examines the challenges that oral historians face when documenting the oral histories of people who have experienced, or are still experiencing, conflict, such as the people of Iraq.[1] Since the beginning of the 1980s, Iraq has been experiencing major upheavals and political, economic, social, and cultural transformations, including a decade-long war with Iran in the 1980s, the Gulf War of 1990–1991, the economic sanctions from 1990 to 2003, and the 2003 invasion and occupation, followed by the current sectarian strife and massive displacement of populations. Upheavals create distrust and distance between human beings. Therefore, documenting oral histories in such times poses unique sets of challenges: How can oral historians gain the trust of the narrators with whom they have to engage in an intimate and fruitful conversation? Oral history is a dialogic discourse created by both the narrators and the oral historian; how can the historians persuade the narrators, who are justifiably suspicious, to open up and tell them what they went through and to continue telling them? How

---

1   I owe thanks to the Women Forum and Memory for inviting me to participate in their international conference on "Oral History in Times of Change: Gender, Documentation and the Making of Archives," in Cairo, Egypt, and to the Supreme Council for Culture in Cairo for hosting me during the conference. I am also grateful to Beth Kangas, a friend and colleague from TAARII, for her insightful comments on an earlier version of this work. My heartfelt gratitude goes to all the Iraqi men and women who told me their life stories in times of serious conflict. The research team of Khizama al-Rasheed, Nawal Ghazawi, and Najwa Adra played a major role in documenting the oral history of Iraqis.

113

can the historians assure their narrators that their narratives will not put them at risk? Finally, why is oral history the most convenient and sensitive tool to understand conflict?

My discussion of these questions is informed by my documentation of the oral histories of Iraqis who migrated to Jordan, Yemen, and Lebanon after decades of wars, invasion, and sectarian conflict. From 2005 to 2009, I was the senior researcher for the Iraqi Oral History Project of The American Academic Research Institute in Iraq (TAARII), a consortium of American universities.[2] The research team conducted 180 interviews with Iraqis living in six different countries (Canada, Jordan, Lebanon, Turkey, the US, and Yemen), representing a broad spectrum of Iraqi society.

The Significance of Oral History

Oral history can be broadly defined as the recording, preservation, and interpretation of historical information, based on the narrators' personal experiences and opinions. In other words, it is a "history built around people" (Thompson 2000:28), or more specifically around marginal groups, such as working classes, ethnic communities, and women, whose voices are usually silenced in the dominant histories. Oral history is a multi-genre; it includes, in addition to oral narratives, folklore, songs, myths, poetry, and stories passed down orally over time. Cultures such as those of the Middle East and North Africa (MENA) region, known for their public and long-term oral traditions, have transmitted the histories of their various communities through oral recitation. The Bani Hilal Epic, known in Arabic as *Sirat* (or *Taghribat*) *Bani Hilal*, which recounts the migration journey of an Arabian tribe from their homeland in Hadramawt, South Yemen, to North Africa in the eleventh century, was passed down orally for a long time before it was committed to writing in relatively recent times. The same is true of the folk tales that are compiled in what is now known as *One Thousand and One Nights*. The histories of Arab tribes, their feuds, wars, and political positions, were, and in some cases still are, transmitted orally and passed down in poetry (for examples, see Sowayan 1985; Shryock 1997; and Taminian 1999).

An oral historical narrative is the product of the process of remembering, which is constantly reconstructed in such a way that some

---

[2] The project was funded by the National Endowment for the Humanities (NEH) of the US.

memories are silenced, others fade away, others are accentuated, and still others are reworked. Oral history is thus concerned with examining the "dynamic nature" of the process of remembering, usually permeated with narrators' silences, the intertwining of their past and present, their use of the past to interpret their world, and their sense of historical consciousness (Hamilton and Shopes 2008; Frisch 1990). For example, the Palestinian narratives of the Deir Yaseen massacre committed by the Zionist military in 1948, which were transmitted orally before being documented, shape the Palestinian political consciousness and their national identity. In other words, the voicing of individual narratives can shape collective memory and identity. Mohaqqeq (2012:4) argues that Afghan women, who are forgotten in the country's history and have internalized the belief that "they have no agency," can reconstruct their suppressed identity and regain their agency by creating their own narratives through oral history.

Portelli (1991; 1997) stresses that oral history is not about what people remember, but about how and why they remember, or the meaning of people's recollection. What is remembered and what is being selectively silenced constitute a comment on the present and/or an expression of an ideological position or national identity (Abu Lughod 1993; Al-Ali 2007; Davis 2011; Slyomovics 1998). These ideological positions and national/cultural identities are extremely important in terms of understanding conflict and rapid changes and in exploring the remembering of events and the creating of meaning.

Memory is not a passive deposit of facts; rather, it is an active process of creating meaning. This process depends mainly upon interest and willingness to remember. On the other hand, remembering can be prevented by unwillingness due to a conscious avoidance of distasteful facts or unconscious repression. For example, in her work on Italians' memories of fascism, Passerini states that her interviewees' recollections of fascism oscillate between "silence and censorship on the one hand, and the recall of the minutest, almost 'insignificant' episodes on the other hand." She argues that "memory resorts to tricks and leaps in time" (2009:67). This is especially noticeable in discussions of ideological positions, because her interviewers identify fascism with evil and a source of national shame and consequently desire to keep silent about it. Her interviewees, therefore, tend to talk about an everyday life that does not bear an obvious imprint of fascism. Similarly, in recounting their experience of violence and wars, Iraqi narrators tend to keep silent about the sectarian violence that erupted after 2006. Talking about this violence is seen as a counter-narrative to the dominant ideology of national unity that they prefer to stress. In addition, men who worked for the Americans after the invasion of Iraq kept silent about their experience to avoid being labeled as traitors.

Scholars have become increasingly aware that oral history, as a linguistic and dialogic event, is one of the most acutely sensitive instruments that they have to understand the complex causes, as well as the consequences, of human conflicts. Through oral history, ordinary people seek to understand the upheavals and changes that they experience in their own lives, and refugees and the displaced try to hold onto and sustain their culture (Thompson 2000; Humphreys 2008). Oral history can have a major role in analyzing patterns of change as they emerge in narrative form, as well as in probing the silences that fragment narratives and prevent the transmission of oral stories into popular as well as historical memory. Recording the oral histories of Iraqis and their family, kin, and social relations for over five generations revealed changes in the social fabric of the neighborhoods of the city of Baghdad, from semi-homogeneous kin-centered groups to heterogeneous communities based on professions, such as teachers', officers', and doctors' neighborhoods. It also showed the fragmentation process of Iraqi families during the last three decades due to wars, sanctions, invasion, and ethnic conflict. When talking about the place of residence of members of their families, Iraqis would say *itashrana*, meaning 'we are scattered all over,' naming the various foreign countries where each member of the family lives. The oral history of Iraqis also revealed changes in social relations, in gender roles, marriage patterns, and identities.

As mentioned above, oral history tells us less about the events than about their meaning. This does not mean that oral history has no factual validity. Interviews can reveal unknown events or unknown aspects of known events; they always cast new light on unexpected areas of daily life. The Iraqi women's narratives about marriages within their extended families over three to five generations revealed changes in sectarian relations over more than 60 years, a sensitive topic that was, and still is, not spoken of. Up to the 1950s, the majority of marriages were endogamous, marrying within one's sect; over the next two decades, exogamous marriages, marrying outside one's sect group, became common. Marrying within one's group solidifies the group's boundaries vis-à-vis the others, whereas marrying outside one's group pushes social organization outward and creates and maintains relationships of affinity, thus linking groups into larger social units. The eruption of sectarian conflict after 2006 turned neighborhoods and towns into sectarian enclaves and many mixed marriages ended in divorce. To encourage mixed marriage, a well-off politician offered financial aid to young men and women who married outside their own sectarian groups after the start of conflict.

Oral history pays special attention to the speaker's subjectivity, "the cultural forms and processes by which individuals express their sense of themselves in history" (Portelli 1991:ix). In other words the "unique and precious element" of oral history is "the speaker's subjectivity," for it allows oral historians to ask not only about the events, but also about the narrators' feelings toward these events, and it allows the narrators to relate their viewpoints of these events (Portelli 1981:107). For example, Iraqis' reflections on the economic sanctions were powerful, though brief. Their views, expressed in short sentences—such as *"al-hisar damar al-Iraq"* ('the sanctions destroyed Iraq'), *"damar hayatna"* ('they destroyed our lives'), and *"al-hisar aswa' men kul al-hurub"* ('the sanctions were worse than all the wars')—are very telling. The narrative of an Iraqi teacher who resigned because her salary was not enough to buy a dozen eggs during the sanctions, and her refusal to take bribes from her students to supplement her income, reveals the complexity of the sanctions' impacts: the spread of corruption due to impoverishment on one hand, and the willpower of Iraqis to resist the devastating impacts of sanctions on the other.

Challenges

The most serious challenge that oral historians face in documenting oral histories in times of conflict relates to the state of mind and emotional well-being of the narrators and their willingness to talk. The documenting of Iraqi oral histories began during a time of suspicion and mistrust among Iraqis living inside and outside Iraq. Many Iraqis in the diaspora feared that they (or their families still in Iraq) would be targeted if information in their interviews were to leak out. Rumors circulating among Iraqis in Jordan, a country neighboring Iraq, intensified their insecurity. On the other hand, a number of Iraqi public figures and/or politicians who were assigned responsibility for the conflict welcomed the opportunity to communicate their counter-narratives in opposition to the dominant narratives circulating in the international, as well as regional and local, media. Oral historians have to be ready to deal with both the rejection and the eagerness of their narrators. Before an interview, historians have to think of the reassurances that they can give to narrators that their interviews will not endanger their lives, and they have to learn about the background of the narrators in order to be prepared to ask both informed and challenging questions.

Another challenge that oral historians often face is the narrators' perception of history. How does the community whose oral histories the historian wants to document perceive history? Do they see any historicity in their private life? History is usually seen as a faraway sphere distant from the daily lives of its people (Portelli 2003:9). When telling Iraqis that I was interested in documenting their oral histories, the response I received from most of them was: "Iraqi history is known. It is written and published." Others, especially women, would insist that their life histories have no historical value, saying "I don't think my life history adds to the history of Iraq." The response raises two issues: first, the belief of 'people,' particularly marginal groups, that they do not have a voice in history, which raises the questions of "How historical is private life?" and "How personal is history?" Portelli argues that oral history "expresses the awareness of the historicity of personal experience and of the individual's role in the history of society and in public events: wars, revolutions, strikes, floods, etc." (1997:6). The second issue is the distortions of memory, perpetrated by a master historical narrative, the popular press, and the media, and created by political forces. The history of modern Iraq was dominated by a master historical narrative, which foregrounded a trajectory of Arab national dominance from the period of the Islamic conquest until the Ba'thist takeover in the 1960s. This master narrative even filtered the history of ancient Mesopotamia through the same ethno-nationalist lens. Iraqis learned this grand narrative at school and constantly encountered it in the media, on billboards, and elsewhere. This narrative shaped the collective memory of Iraqis for decades; alternative narratives were marginal and delegitimized. Only by assuring Iraqis that

I was interested in documenting the sociocultural history of Iraq, including the life histories of their families, their neighborhoods, and so on, and the impact of conflict on their lives, thus depoliticizing and humanizing the interview, did I gain the trust of the narrators and was able to convince them that they have a historical voice.

Ethics and Standards of Practice: The Interview

Oral history, as mentioned before, is a dialogic discourse, created not only by what the historian says, but by what the historian and narrator do together at the moment of their encounter in the interview (Portelli 1997:3). In other words, the final result of the interview is the product of both the narrator and the historian. The quality of the product depends largely on the degree of rapport established, which allows for an exchange of ideas, values, and different types of knowledge. A dialogical interview is flexible and depends more on a dialogue format (for example, "I'm interested in learning about your life" or "Can you tell me about your life?") and less on a questionnaire ("When were you born? Where?" etc.). A dialogue format may reveal aspects of the conflict unknown to historians, which may turn out to be worth pursuing. An open dialogic communication is characterized by openness, mutual respect, trust, equality, and a joint interest in the creation of narratives.

A productive interview depends on the narrators' willingness to talk freely about their experiences, which in turn depends on the willingness of oral historians to reveal their identity and to answer openly the narrators' questions about their background, thoughts, and so on. The more they reveal, the more engaging narrators become; the less revealing the historian, the more the narrators stick to the official aspects of their experience of conflict. Oral historians have to bear in mind that narrators are as curious as they are to know about their interlocutors. When I introduced myself to the Iraqi narrators, they would become inquisitive about my background, the history of my family, and how I as an Armenian had come to live in Jordan. The telling of my family history would create a bond based on shared experience of conflict and displacement; thus, the interview would turn into an intimate conversation and the narrators would talk about their experiences in depth.

To gain the respect of their narrators, oral historians need to demonstrate sufficient knowledge of the subject under discussion. Doing some research on the recent history of Iraq and Iraqi society and culture helped me to ask informed questions and to engage in an animated conversation with my narrators, thereby gaining their respect. An essential requirement for a productive conversation is the historians' respect for their narrators. Giving the narrators a chance to respond freely to their questions, listening attentively to their narration, showing interest in their narratives, and respecting their views will generate self-confidence in the narrators and encourage them to open up and speak freely. When narrators neglect to answer historians' questions and choose instead to talk for a long time about irrelevant matters, the oral historian should listen and wait, saving any unanswered questions for another interview.

Equality is a condition for establishing rapport with narrators and for a credible interview. Equality does not negate differences between oral historians and narrators (Portelli 1991:31). It requires being sensitive to differences between themselves and their narrators, such as age, class, educational level, nationality, and religion, and at the same time being aware of their dependence on the narrators in order to gain the knowledge that they pursue and stimulate a productive dialogue. On the other hand, the narrators' realization that their life histories are important for understanding conflict enhances their authority and self-awareness, and may encourage them to speak about aspects of their experiences that they have never spoken about or even seriously thought about (Portelli 1997:4).

In conflict situations, talking can put the lives of narrators or others at risk, and they might intentionally keep silent about certain aspects to protect themselves, family members, or friends. Historians have to respect their silence and can either reformulate their questions or avoid asking them, but nevertheless silences have meaning. When asked about the events they experienced, Iraqis would present the 'official' narrative that was not fraught with danger. However, when asked about the impact of these events on their own lives, their families, and their communities, the narrators talked much more freely. An Iraqi who mentioned in passing that he lived in the Green Zone after 2003 ignored my questions about his experience living there. This could mean that there have been changes in his consciousness; acts considered normal in the past might be viewed at the time of the interview as unacceptable.

Finally, oral history is an ethical process that involves respecting the rights and dignity of the narrators. Protecting narrators who have experienced wars and conflict from any anticipated risks and obtaining their 'informed consent' are basic ethical codes. Another key principle is to inform narrators of their rights to the recordings, to allow them to review the transcriptions, and to obtain their approval to use them. It is necessary to mask their identities if they choose to, and to store the recordings and transcripts in a secure place.

Conclusion

Reflecting on the conflict and hostilities that Iraq has been experiencing for more than three decades, Najem Wali, an Iraqi novelist based in Germany, argues that the Iraq he knows has been *"indathara,"* meaning 'wiped out,' and "nothing remained of its past except anecdotes and narratives."[3] The term *indathara* resonates with two other terms mentioned above and repeated by many narrators: *iddmarna* and *itasharna*. The three terms express the narrators' subjectivity, and tell about their feelings towards the loss of an Iraq they lived in, the destruction of their lives, and the breakdown of their family relations and their social networks.

In his book *The Invisible Cities*, Calvino points out that cities' past is written in "redundant signs," that are repeated so that "something will stick in mind," and that memory is redundant in the sense that "it repeats these signs so that city can begin to exist" (1978:11, 19). The process of remembering and telling about their cities, villages, and schools they attended as well as their painful experience of destruction and loss made the life the Iraqi narrators desire and long for imaginable.

References

Abu Lughod, Lila. 1993. *Writing Women's Worlds: Bedouin Stories*. Berkeley: University of California Press.

Al-Ali, Nadje. 2007. *Iraqi Women: Untold Stories from 1948 to the Present*. London and New York: Zed Books.

Calvino, Italo. 1978. *Invisible Cities*. W. Weaver, trans. San Diego: Harvest Books.

---

3   Najem Wali, "Mantiqah Muhrarah: Ana almuwatin min Babel," *al-Mada Newspaper*, 2017, Issue 3931.

Davis, Rochelle. 2011. *Palestinian Village Histories: Geographies of the Displaced*. Stanford, CA: Stanford University Press.

Frisch, Michael. 1990. *A Shared Authority: Essays on the Craft and Meaning of Oral and Public History*. Albany: State University of New York Press.

Hamilton, P., and L. Shopes. 2008. "Introduction." In *Oral History and Public Memories*, vii–xvii. Philadelphia: Temple University Press.

Humphreys, Isabelle. 2008. "Listening to the Displaced Narrative: Politics, Power, and Grassroots Communication amongst Palestinians inside Israel," *Middle East Journal of Culture and Communication*, 1(2): 180–196.

Mohaqqeq, Mohammad. 2012. "The Possibilities of Oral History in Situations of Conflict." In M. C. Clark et al., eds. *Documenting and Interpreting Conflict through Oral History: A Working Guide*, 4–5. Columbia University Center for Oral History Research. http://library.columbia.edu/content/dam/libraryweb/locations/ohro/Documenting_and_Interpreting_Conflict_Through_Oral_History.pdf

Passerini, Luisa. 2009. *Fascism in Popular Memory: The Cultural Experience of the Turin Working Class*. R. Lumely and J. Bloomfield, trans. Digitally printed version.

Portelli, Alessandro. 1981. "The Peculiarities of Oral History," *History Workshop Journal*, 12(1): 96–107.

———. 1991. *The Death of Luigi Trastulli and Other Stories: Form and Meaning in Oral History*. Albany: State University of New York Press.

———. 1997. *The Battle of Valle Giulia: Oral History and the Art of Dialogue*. Madison: University of Wisconsin Press.

———. 2003. *The Order Has Been Carried Out: History, Memory and Meaning of a Nazi Massacre in Rome*. New York: Palgrave Macmillan.

Shryock, Andrew. 1997. *Nationalism and the Genealogical Imagination: Oral History and Textual Authority in Tribal Jordan*. Comparative Studies on Muslim Societies 23. Berkeley: University of California Press.

Slyomovics, Susan.1998. *The Object of Memory: Arab and Jew Narrate the Palestinian Village*. Philadelphia: University of Pennsylvania Press.

Sowayan, S. Abdullah. 1985. *Nabati Poetry: The Oral Poetry of Arabia*. Berkeley: University of California Press.

Taminian, Lucine. 1999. "Persuading the Monarchs: Poetry and Politics in Yemen." In R. Leveu et al., eds. *Le Yemen Contemporain*, 203–219. Paris: Editions Karthala.

Thompson, Paul. 2000. *The Voice of the Past: Oral History*. 3rd ed. Oxford and New York: Oxford University Press.

CHAPTER 9

Testimonio as Methodology: Archiving, Translating, and Theorizing Egyptian Women's Experiences of Gendered Violence in the January 25th Revolution

Manal Hamzeh

Introduction

This chapter is part of the current theoretical questioning of gender justice within the 'Arab Spring' field of research (El Said, Meari, and Pratt 2015; Hafez 2014; Khalil 2014, 2015; Morsy 2014). It discusses the methodology of *testimonio* within the context of the January 25th Revolution. *Testimonio*, as a methodology, guided a transnational Arab feminist study to archive, translate, and theorize Egyptian women's embodied experiences of gendered state violence. This critical qualitative research project centered on several televised *testimonios*, or public accounts, of four Egyptian women who experienced gendered state violence at crucial moments in the past few years.

This project started when I visited Cairo in December 2011 to learn about the January 25th Revolution first-hand. It was a very charged moment. My visit fell between two major events at the end of 2011, including the event that highlighted the public beating and dragging of a woman protestor dubbed 'the girl with the blue bra.' This is when I spontaneously began to collect *testimonios* attending to the urgency of the stories and calls of Egyptian women, especially those who experienced gendered state violence (Flores Carmona 2014).

I felt this was a moment at which I could extend my scholarship to a more creative, transborder, translanguage, and political journey, despite my geographical distance from Egypt. As a decolonizing feminist, I acted in solidarity with Egyptian women (Mohanty 2003) by committing to publish and teach their *testimonios*, because according to

Kathryn Reyes and Julia Rodríguez *testimonios* are "intimate" accounts that are "not meant to be hidden . . . nor kept secret" (2012:525). This was a response to Ruth Trinidad Galván's call for countering "the global processes that serve as recolonizing practices" (2014:138).

In the first part of this chapter, I situate *testimonio* theoretically and methodologically in feminist epistemologies and discuss its role in this project. Then I discuss *testimonio*'s power and potential reflected in the analysis so far.[1]

Theoretical Framing

In this project, I drew on the commitments of transnational feminisms (Mohanty 2003, 2013; Moghadam 2013; Naber 2011; Nagar 2014; Salime 2014) to an 'anti-imperialist praxis' anchored in a politics of dissent (Mohanty 2006:7). I also used transnational feminist theoretical notions and practices of 'cross-border and situated solidarities,' 'insurgent knowledges,' and 'anti-racist, anti-imperial praxis' (Mohanty 2003; Nagar 2014). Thus, this is a solidarity-centered project aiming to engage feminist knowledge reflexively with Egyptian women within transborder and transnational social movements struggling against global capitalism, militarism, and imperialism (Mohanty 2003, 2013). At the core of this project is the Chicana *feminista* tradition of theorizing (Anzaldúa 1987; Moraga and Anzaldúa 1983; Salime 2014) from "the brown female body, breaking silences, and bearing witness to both injustices and social change" (Delgado Bernal, Burciaga, and Flores Carmona 2012:364).

Methodology

Driven by the above theoretical framing, I used both *testimonio* and translation to methodologically guide this study. First, *testimonio* as a methodology is different from interviewing, oral history, and narrations. As public accounts of injustice, they are intentionally political. *Testimonios*' roots are in South and Central America. Reyes and Rodríguez explain that *testimonios* were accounts of anti-militarist and anti-imperialist struggles in the 1970s with a collective goal of building

---

1 The author is in the process of completing the tasks of archiving, translating, and analyzing the *testimonios* that are the subject of this chapter in an academic book and a graphic documentary book, due to be published by the end of 2018.

up a "discourse of solidarity" (2012:526). Later, Chicanas and Latinas transformed *testimonio* as a methodology working with liberation pedagogy and being influenced by Black Feminists' "deliberate use of personal theoretical insights" (2012:525). "The cornerstone of *testimonio*, like oral history, is not the speaking of truth, but rather, the telling of an account from an individual point of view whose consciousness has led to an analysis of the experience as a shared component of oppression" (2012:528).

The *testimonios* of four Egyptian women are the main data for this project. They are the immediate, first-person, self-conscious, and narrated accounts of their oppression. The women's *testimonios* also guided my methodology and the narrative that I developed out of them. As Reyes and Rodríguez note, *testimonios* are an urgent "practice of reflexive narratives of liberation used by people throughout the world" (2012:525).

Second, I used translation as a feminist methodology to construct a "testimonial text" (Reyes and Rodrigues 2012:526). This use of *testimonio* troubles ways that the academy, media, and think tanks, mainly in the West, produce and disseminate knowledge about Arab women and the so-called 'Arab Spring' (El Said, Meari, and Pratt 2015). I used translation as an ongoing and urgent political praxis necessary to explore the power and potential of Egyptian women's Arabic *testimonios*. Thus, methodologically, I took these *testimonios* from their oral and visual forms to their transcribed and written form, in Arabic and English, in order to "bring to light a wrong, a point of view or an urgent call for action" (Reyes and Rodríguez 2012:525).

With my commitments and praxis in this project, I have built 'situated' solidarities with the narrators and activists' communities in Egypt and have in many ways contested the cross-border configuration of state-supported gendered violence (Nagar 2014). This means I began doing some necessary work to decolonize knowledge production, which is at the core of transnational feminist struggles (Mohanty 2013). Doing the decolonizing and cross-border work in this project, I was also aware of vulnerabilities and risks, which were not just intellectual and political, but also 'affects' in my skin, my bone, my flesh, and in my deepest, ethical core, and were at the heart of the textual narrative developed out of the study.

Positionalities of the Researcher

In this project, I acted as an anti-racist, Arab feminist, born in Jordan. I am a product of an anti-colonial home education and a long familial political history with Egypt. I feel that I am organically *homed* in Egypt and its revolution. My first language is Arabic and I use it as an empowering tool. I used my literacies of Arabic and Egyptian history and politics at every stage of the project. I have also been living in exile since 2003 and teaching social justice education and gender studies in a US university. In these positionalities, the tasks of this project came with certain responsibilities. I was entrusted to listen deeply to Egyptian women's pain and dreams and to bear witness to the oppression they experienced. Thus, I was entrusted to teach and disseminate these *testimonios* that exposed and talked back to oppression and opened ways for practices of resistance and social change (Flores Carmona 2014). So, taking the role of translating the *testimonios* of Egyptian women from Egyptian Arabic into English, I was an in-betweener. With this translation, I have also bridged their *testimonios* (Flores Carmona 2014) as contextualized textual narratives to an English-speaking public in the North (Trinidad Galván 2014).

Methods and Data Sources

I used various sources of data. First, I purposefully selected (Hesse-Biber 2013) the *testimonios* of a number of young Egyptian women, who were assaulted at four crucial moments—Women's International Day protests in Tahrir, March 2011; *Ahdath Majles al-Wuzara*, December 2011; *Ahdath Qasr al-Itihadiya*, November 2012; and *Ahdath Majles al-Shura*, November 2013. Second, I used relevant online sources to contextualize the selected *testimonios* (1–3 hours each) in the context of the January 25th Revolution. The online sources included tweets of the narrators; prominent activists' tweets during the '18 days' of the revolution; and related tweets and hashtags.

I draw on Facebook newsfeeds, online photos, photos of graffiti, cartoons, articles, and YouTube videos. My data included reports and documents of Egyptian legal and civil-rights NGOs. I used the narrators' interviews on non-state-owned Egyptian TV and the footage of one feature film about the journey of one of the main narrators, *Trails of Spring* (2015). Finally, I interviewed the narrators personally in Cairo, in the US, or via Skype for 1–4 hours each.

Analysis

All sources of data were in Arabic. I transcribed the main *testimonios* material, from their oral form, into Arabic script, typed them, and then translated them into English. This is a more complex process than mere transcribing; it involved more of a conceptual translation, paying attention to "subtle issues of connotation and meaning" (Flores Carmona 2014:117). This part of the analysis process required persistent critical self-reflexivity throughout the project to assure that the English wording is not "unjust or harmful to the narrators and to the language" (Flores Carmona 2014:117).

More importantly, in the latter part of the analysis process, I retranslated the textual narratives of the *testimonios* into Arabic in order to share them with the narrators and for them to edit/rewrite as they saw fit in their own lives and from their perspective. This is part of the struggle to find a shared agenda throughout the official and unofficial duration of the project. I am committed to this solidarity method of analysis as alliance work that moves through and across different contexts and spaces. It is the alliance that "does not merely include the work of writing but the ways that writing is informed—and coauthored—by all the processes and events undertaken by everybody involved" (Nagar 2014:3732).

Throughout the project, I used all kinds of tools in order to be faithful to the responsibilities with which I was entrusted. I was aware that my positionalities worked hand-in-hand with critical self-reflexivity in an evolving process over time and location/space (Hesse-Biber 2013). Thus, I engaged with the possibilities as well as the impossibilities of the translations as an evolving practice of building trust with the narrators and holding on to the faith in the power of *testimonios*. At the same time, I stayed reflexive and engaged with the questions of power and privilege, mediation, translation, and representation and took them as constructive challenges, as well as political possibilities, to cultivate "an alliance of transnational actors" (Nagar 2014:2923–2926). That is, I was aware that the *testimonios* I was translating were "fragments of" these Egyptian women's "experiences making this work messier and myself more radically vulnerable" (Nagar 2014:984). The complex, evolving process of translation continued to be an ethical practice always guided by my passion for justice and inspired by Egyptian women's spirit of resistance.

This project is in keeping with the *feminista* and transnational feminist methodologies of foregrounding marginalized voices of brown colonized women. It represents my sustained commitment to learn directly from the selected Egyptian narrators and to center their *testimonios* in the archiving and publication parts of the project. The final forms of this project will be a book, in English, and a graphic documentary book, in both Arabic and English. Both forms will be built on 'coauthored' work with the selected narrators of the *testimonios*. While the book will include their Arabic and English *testimonios* as well as my textual narrative about them, the graphic documentary book will be built on the actual selected *testimonios* in their original video and textual forms. Thus, at the end, this project will be a larger, multifaceted, solidarity-centered, transnational, feminist praxis guided by transborder Arab and Chicana feminist epistemologies, methodologies, and solidarities.

The Power and Potential of *Testimonios*

As a result of the analysis completed so far, I claim that the *testimonios* in this project acted as a powerful conduit for silenced *truths* to be spoken. As the Egyptian women spoke their bodily experiences, they made publicly visible the systemic oppressive practices of a patriarchal, militarist, Islamist, neoliberal, and neocolonial nexus (Khalil 2014). As 'experiential reflections' of Egyptian women on collective gendered experiences, these *testimonios* also presented new non-normative forms of embodied resistance and further asserted their critical subversive potential (Hafez 2014). Publicized via visual online, the *testimonios* in this project were examples of subversive practices that opened new spaces for freedom, equity, and justice. As a result, these *testimonios* have publicly disrupted gendered violence instigated by what is thought of as an unshakable patriarchal nexus of forces in Egypt. Evidently, they have mobilized unprecedented solidarity campaigns addressing sexual violence against women and seeking justice (Delgado Bernal, Burciaga, and Flores Carmona 2012).

The *testimonios* selected for this project have a wide political and pedagogical reach in Egypt and other Arab-speaking contexts. They were embodied experiences spoken in Egyptian Arabic, using TV and the Internet as both visual and auditory channels of communication. These *testimonios* were an accumulation of Egyptian women's visceral knowledge and practices of resistance. They were achievements of new knowledge and practices of sustenance tactics against the relentless brutality they are still facing at this time. These *testimonios* were also Egyptian women's means of the conscientization and empowerment (Reyes and Rodríguez 2012) necessary to continue a long journey toward the goals of the Revolution—dignity, freedom, and social justice. These evolving visceral knowledges and practices of Egyptian women represent the centrality of "gendered corporeality" in the Revolution (Hafez 2014:184).

The Egyptian women's *testimonios* of lived oppression or "cathartic confession," in the words of Flores Carmona, were used as tools that have the potential "to stop the silences and demand listening" (2014:118). They were potentially part of a collective revolutionary consciousness (Freire 1990). In other words, these *testimonios* represent the voices of many other women who have experienced state-inflicted gendered violence in the past few years in Egypt. They form a collective story or a 'collective empowerment' for all who could relate to such oppressive experiences, and they are many in Egypt. To the Latina Feminist Group, such *testimonios* are "disclosures not of personal lives but rather of the political violence inflicted on whole communities" (Latina Feminist Group 2001, cited in Flores Carmona 2014:118).

On another level, these *testimonios* have the potential to teach new ways of resilience that Egyptian women embody in this time of intense change. Importantly, they embodied a public pedagogy used in creative resistance campaigns within the larger landscape of social movements. The *testimonios* help to inspire and then sustain the intensity of the resistance campaigns. As sources of knowledge, these *testimonios* of Egyptian women and the narratives I have constructed of them also revealed their potential as critical literacy tools capable of naming oppression, as well as interrupting the actions of institutional oppression. With their political intention, the *testimonios* of Egyptian women could also produce "awareness to the listeners and the readers alike" (Reyes and Rodríguez 2012:257)—those who read English or Arabic. The project's disseminated *testimonios* foreground the hybrid and complex lived experiences of women in Egypt. This outcome also discloses the potential to counter the compartmentalized and sensationalized representations of women in Egypt that have proliferated in Western media and are still rarely challenged in the academy (El Said, Meari, and Pratt 2015).

This kind of transnational feminist praxis across languages, scholarships, and activisms is an invitation to English readers to enter into an urgent and critical dialogue with these *testimonios* and what they reveal (Nagar 2014). It is just one humble step toward the more intricate exposure of how regimes operate within the interlocking global systems of racism, colonialism, Islamism, capitalism, heteronormativity, nationalism, and militarism. Finally, as teachable forms of knowledge and critical literacy, these *testimonios* could be used in the classrooms to do necessary decolonizing work, and at the same time, to connect to the learners' racialized experiences in North America. Egyptian women's *testimonios* within the context of the January 25th Revolution are part of an urgent decolonizing feminist methodology and pedagogy in this time of change.

References

Anzaldúa, Gloria. 1987. *Borderlands/la frontera: The New Mestiza*. San Francisco: Aunt Lute Books.

Delgado Bernal, Dolores, Rebeca Burciaga, and Judith Flores Carmona. 2012. "Chicana/Latina Testimonios: Mapping the Methodological, Pedagogical, and Political," *Equity and Excellence in Education*, 45(3): 363–372.

Flores Carmona, Judith. 2014. "Cutting Out Their Tongues: Mujeres' Testimonios and the Malintzin Researcher," *Journal of Latino/Latin American Studies*, 6(2): 113–124.

Freire, Paulo. 1990. *Pedagogy of the Oppressed*. Rev. ed. New York: Continuum.

Hafez, Sherine. 2014. "The Revolution Shall Not Pass through Women's Bodies: Egypt, Uprising and Gender Politics," *Journal of North African Studies*, 19(2): 172–185.

Hesse-Biber, Sharlene Nagy. 2013. *Feminist Research Practice: A Primer*. Thousand Oaks, CA: Sage Publications.

Khalil, Andrea. 2014. "Gender Paradoxes of the Arab Spring," *Journal of North African Studies*, 19(2): 131–136.

———. 2015. "New Texts Out Now: Andrea Khalil, Gender, Women, and the Arab Spring," *Jadaliyya*, February 18. Accessed February 23, 2015. http://www.jadaliyya.com/pages/index/20858/new-texts-out-now_andrea-khalil-gender-women-and-t

Moghadam, Valentine. 2013. "What Is Democracy? Promises and Perils of the Arab Spring," *Current Sociology*, 61(4): 393–408.
Mohanty, Chandra Talpade. 2003. *Feminism without Borders: Decolonizing Theory and Practicing Solidarity*. Durham, NC: Duke University Press.
———. 2006. "US Empire and the Project of Women's Studies: Stories of Citizenship, Complicity and Dissent," *Gender Place and Culture*, 13(1): 7–20.
———. 2013. "Transnational Feminist Crossings: On Neoliberalism and Radical Critique," *Signs: Journal of Women in Culture and Society*, 38(4): 967–991.
Moraga, Cherrie, and Gloria Anzaldúa. 1983. *This Bridge Called My Back: Writings by Radical Women of Color*. New York: Kitchen Table/Women of Color Press.
Morsy, Maya. 2014. "Egyptian Women and the 25th of January Revolution: Presence and Absence," *Journal of North African Studies*, 19(2): 211–229.
Naber, Nadine. 2011. "Imperial Feminism, Islamophobia, and the Egyptian Revolution," *Jadaliyyah*, February 11. Accessed June 10, 2011. http://www.jadaliyya.com/pages/index/616/imperial-feminism-islamophobia-and-the-egyptian-revolution
Nagar, Richa. 2014. *Muddying the Waters: Coauthoring Feminisms across Scholarship and Activism*. Champaign: University of Illinois Press. Kindle edition.
Reyes, Kathryn Blackmer, and Julia E. Curry Rodríguez. 2012. "*Testimonio*: Origins, Terms, and Resources," *Equity and Excellence in Education*, 45(3): 525–538.
El Said, Maha, Lena Meari, and Nicole Pratt. 2015. *Rethinking Gender in Revolution and Resistance: Lessons from the Arab World*. London: Zed Books.
Salime, Zakia. 2014. "New Feminism as Personal Revolutions: Microbellious Bodies," *Signs: Journal of Women in Culture and Society*, 40(1): 14–19.
Trinidad Galván, Ruth. 2014. "Chicana/Latin American Feminist Epistemologies of the Global South (within and outside the North): Decolonizing *El Conocimiento* and Creating Global Alliances," *Journal of Latino/Latin American Studies*, 6(2): 135–140.

IV

Praxis: Entanglements in Two Projects Documenting Gender and Revolution

CHAPTER 10

Narrating Gender in Egypt's Public Sphere: The Archive of Women's Oral History

Maissan Hassan and Diana Magdy

The January 25th Revolution in 2011 marked a major historical transformation in Egypt. While calls for social change were rising, normalized gender roles were being contested. The participation of women in the events of the January Revolution opened up the discussion on the agency of women in the public sphere. Gender power relations were also being negotiated in the private sphere. Women's images as active participants in the major movements of change were seen throughout the upheaval through media coverage and other spaces, yet "visibility does not necessarily mean 'voice' or empowerment" (Hayes 2005:521). Seeing images of women does not provide adequate insights into the understanding of how gender norms are being challenged during the processes of social change. Therefore, the representation of women's experiences in times of change has been a persistent concern for many feminists in Egypt.

Documenting women's experiences remains an essential tool for enriching women's history and supporting the feminist movement. Feminists and women's rights activists use women's narratives, as they provide "an avenue for understanding and documenting women's culture and history" (Gluck and Patai 1991:1). Exploring the gender dimension embedded within these narratives allows us to understand relationships of power. Women's stories aim to challenge cultural stereotypes in an attempt to subvert dominant narratives to effect change. Moreover, collecting women's stories—which highlight their achievements and their strength—in women's archives is empowering to women's rights groups and feminist movements (Elsadda 2016:152).

The Women and Memory Forum

In 1995, the Women and Memory Forum (WMF) was founded in Cairo, Egypt. WMF has been at the forefront of feminist research groups that focus on the documentation, production, and dissemination of alternative knowledge on the history of women in Egypt and across the Arab region. Prior to 2011, WMF worked extensively on establishing a specialized resource center under the name of the Women and Memory Library and Documentation Center (WMLDC) to house historical materials and contemporary research on women's issues and gender equality. The WMLDC focuses on collecting and preserving three types of materials: 1) gray literature (unpublished materials, books with limited circulation and not easily accessible, conference papers, government reports, NGO research pamphlets, flyers, posters, etc.) on gender and women's issues in Egypt and the Arab region; 2) rare books and women's journals and magazines published in the nineteenth and early twentieth centuries; 3) private papers of Egyptian women who played important roles in public life (their personal papers, letters, diaries).

WMF has focused on making alternative feminist knowledge available to researchers, activists, and gender equality advocates as well as to the general public. Linking specialized research and activism has been a persistent goal of WMF. In addition, WMF has actively explored new forms and venues for the dissemination of specialized research to wider audiences. This was the thinking behind a series of illustrated books to introduce an idea or an aspect of women's history. It has also led to what became a defining mark of WMF, the retelling of folktales from a feminist perspective. In this project, traditional folktales were rewritten and published with the view of challenging stereotypical representations of gender in traditional narratives. The stories also became rich material for holding storytelling performances—events which attracted large audiences. WMF has also produced posters of women whose stories have been marginalized from mainstream narratives of history, such as Wedad Mitri, Marie Assaad, Lotfia al-Nady, and Doria Shafik. In 2015, WMF held its first public exhibit: "The Private Papers of Wedad Mitri: A Pioneering Unionist." The exhibit displayed archival materials, photographs, and memorabilia from Mitri's private collection, housed at WMF. The exhibit also included excerpts from an oral narrative by

Mitri. Believing in the potential of documenting women's narratives to enhance the lived realities of women in contemporary societies, WMF initiated its first oral history project in the late 1990s. The Archive of Women's Oral History consists of several collections, such as the Women Pioneers Collection, which includes more than 100 narratives of pioneering women in various walks of life such as social work, art, and politics, and the Women in the Public Sphere Post-2011 Collection.

Over the course of more than two decades, the WMF research group developed into a well-established feminist organization that hosts one of the very few women's archives in the MENA region. After 2011, the work of WMF became extremely significant to the efforts of activists and civil society in Egypt. As a specialized resource center housing alternative histories of Egyptian social movements, WMF archives were inspiring to many activists addressing contemporary issues such the mobilization towards women's representation in the new Egyptian constitutions.

Toward a Post-2011 Feminist Archive

The aftermath of the January 25th Revolution saw a significant increase in documentation projects. Several established organizations as well as newly formed initiatives started to compile photographs and collect stories in order to document political and social changes. Many of these projects were motivated by a desire to safeguard the memory of a major historical event. In addition, they intended to engage with the process of creating well-established narratives on the Tahrir protests. However, few of these projects focused on gender issues and women's experiences.

As feminist researchers and documentarians witnessing and participating in the mobilization of January 2011, members of WMF believed in the necessity of documenting women's experiences during this transformative political moment. Capitalizing on WMF's previous experiences in oral history documentation, the decision was to start documenting the experiences of women, in particular young women under the age of 35, who participated in the Tahrir protests.

In March 2011, WMF started a pilot documentation project to record the lived experiences of these young women by conducting semi-structured interviews. The WMF research team developed a line of inquiry including questions that examined the various problematic issues of women's participation in collective political action and its influence on gender issues in Egyptian society. Researchers started the interviews with questions tracing the narrators' memories of the timeline of events occurring during the sit-in in Tahrir Square, which lasted for 18 days. The line of inquiry also included a set of questions investigating the motivations to participate in the protests and the experiences of engagement with political and social activism before January 25, 2011. A third set of questions focused on perceptions of feminist mobilization and gender relations during the 18 days. Finally, the narrators were asked whether the Revolution contributed to changes in their worldviews. The pilot project consisted of more than 20 interviews with young women who came from various socioeconomic backgrounds and whose ages were between 18 and 35 years. Some of the narrators were politically active before 2011. For others, participating in the Tahrir protests was their first experience of engagement with public life.

The Tahrir protests have not only caused changes in the ruling political regime but have also triggered fundamental political and social change that is worth documenting and examining. This change was being manifested in many women's attempts to contest hegemonic gender roles. In the months following the Tahrir sit-in, mobilization of women in informal and formal politics as well as feminist and women's rights groups increased significantly. At the same time, women, in particular young women, became more outspoken about their frustration with the status of women in Egypt. Many of the narratives recorded during the pilot phase addressed how the narrators broke many 'taboos' of Egyptian society, such as speaking against sexual harassment and defying families' authority over women's professional and personal decisions.

The interviews, conducted between April and August 2011, revealed a few recurrent themes on how the events of the Revolution affected the personal experiences of the narrators and later influenced their decisions regarding career choices and personal relationships. While many of the interviews reflected hope and aspiration in spite of increasing challenges, some narrators expressed deep concerns over the path toward democracy and social justice in Egypt. In addition, the oral narratives addressed issues of gender-based violence and gender relations within families, for example the narrators' experiences of negotiations with their families for permission to participate in the protest. Interestingly, many of the recorded narratives addressed the increasing tension between feminist demands and calls for gender equality on one hand and the demands for social and political justice on another.

The recorded oral narratives provided various personal accounts about a shared political experience. Different narrators emphasized different events. For some, witnessing the eruption of violence was a central theme in their memories of the sit-in. Others described the sit-in as a utopian-like community that was harmonious and just. Most of the young women narrators spoke of the sit-in as a life-changing experience. Interestingly, their experiences varied greatly. The Tahrir sit-in was the first time for many narrators to closely interact with individuals with opposing political affiliations. On the other hand, the protests were the trigger for many narrators to take major professional and personal decisions. Most of the narrators expressed an increasing sense of belonging to Egypt and a growing belief in the power of collective action.

Guided by the preliminary insights gathered during the pilot phase, and drawing on the experience of documenting life stories of women pioneers in the public sphere, the project was modified, and continues to be revised in order to address the rapid political transformations post-2011. Reflecting on the feedback the WMF team received was essential in developing the project into a major oral history archive. The line of inquiry was adjusted in response to the changing political situation in Egypt. New questions were added to allow the narrators to share their memories of events occurring after 2011. During the interviews, the questions were also modified according to the activism experience of each narrator. In addition to changes in the line of inquiry, the selection criterion of narrators was broadened to include women from different age groups as well as from various geographical locations in Egypt. The research team included Hoda Elsadda, Maissan Hassan, Diana Magdy, Omnia Khalil, Dalia Ebeid, Aya Sami, Alia al-Ryan, Hana Shaltout, and Salma Abdel Salam, some members joining at different stages of the project. The research team was supported by an administrative team including Dalia el-Hamamsy, Ramy Ryad, Amira Nady, Nahla Salama, and Marina Gorgy. More than 100 oral narratives were documented and made available in the Women in the Public Sphere Post-2011 Collection.

Notes on the Interviewing Process and Methodology

The main research question for the Post-2011 Collection was how the political changes after 2011 affected women's lives and experiences. Sub-questions investigated themes of power, authority, violence, and women's agency. The questions also explored how the personal intersected with the public. For instance, the questions addressed how the narrators' political experiences affected their relationships with families, friends, and colleagues, and how these experiences influenced their personal and professional choices. The interviews also provided the narrators with a space to reflect on their relationship with the street and to what extent concepts of fear, violence, and safety are experienced in public space. Other questions encouraged the narrators to explore their perceptions of the status of women before and after the Revolution and whether being women affected their experiences as participants and leaders in the movements for change.

The selection of narrators was based on a number of criteria, the main one being substantial participation in the public sphere post-2011. This included women who joined political parties, NGOs, and unions, as well as women who founded informal cultural, political, or social initiatives. To ensure diversity of experiences, additional criteria, such as age, class, and geographical location, guided the selection process.

Most of the interviews were conducted between January and December 2014 in Cairo. The research team was able to collect and document stories with more than 25 narrators from different governorates, such as Alexandria, Port Said, Ismailiya, Bahariya, Luxor, and Aswan. Narrators from outside Cairo were often members or co-founders of young feminist initiatives that emerged after 2011.

As feminist researchers collecting personal narratives about shared political experiences, we were committed to adopting a feminist approach in the interviews. In "Learning to Listen: Interview Techniques and Analysis," Anderson and Jack emphasize the importance of approaching the interviews as interactive processes instead of mere means to gather data. They also suggest techniques for challenging preconceived notions during a feminist oral history interview (Anderson and Jack 1991). These techniques include acknowledging the variations among narrators in using language. In addition, they emphasize the need for researchers to listen to themselves during the interviews in order to mark areas of confusion and discomfort. They noted that sharing the interviews with other researchers during the research process was instrumental in refining their interviewing techniques (1991:11–26). Reflecting on the recorded interviews is an example of a self-critical approach, which is essential in the reciprocal process of feminist oral history. Sharlene Nagy Hesse-Biber argues that reflexivity will help the researchers acknowledge their different roles in the research project and overcome the challenges caused by these roles (2013:216).

In order to encourage reflexivity among members of the research team working on the Women in the Public Sphere Post-2011 Collection, researchers were asked to write field notes and share them during the weekly team meetings. These meetings provided a space for discussion, reflection, and learning. The researchers reflected on biases and areas of discomfort that arose during the interviews. Team members regularly shared excerpts from the recorded narratives during the meetings. Most importantly, the researchers not only discussed the recorded interview but also shared reflections on the encounter with the narrators. For instance, the team reflected extensively on their roles as feminist researchers-activists conducting feminist oral history while being aware of the narrators' various views on feminism in Egypt. This reflection led to refining the researchers' interviewing techniques, especially for questions exploring the narrators' views on gender issues.

After the interviews, women narrators are involved in making decisions on the accessibility of their narratives to users of WMF archives and the general public. During the interviews, consent forms on conducting and further sharing of the interviews are presented to the narrators. The forms introduce the research project, its scope, and its different phases. As a follow-up, the edited transcripts and short abstracts are shared with the narrators, who have the right to review and edit the text before it is made available in the archives. Respecting the narrators' wishes has been a major ethical concern for the research team. The wishes of the narrators are always respected and they have control over the conditions of accessibility.

Due to the political turmoil Egypt has been facing since 2011 and the temporality embedded in the nature of oral narratives, the collected narratives sometimes varied greatly depending on the date of the interview. Among the questions facing the research team were the nature of the archive we are building and the emotions characterizing its narratives. Are we collecting memories of an imagined utopia? Are we recording elegies of lost dreams? Or are we documenting moments of hope and stories of resistance? How to contextualize stories of success as well as stories of disappointment? Most importantly, how to build a feminist archive that would support social change, and how to envision the potential role of this archive in the future?

On a practical level, the political situation in Egypt resulted in frequent interruptions in the documentation process. The team members have been working in an unpredictable, highly politically charged situation that had an emotional impact on the narrators as well as on the researchers. In addition, the process of interviewing, including the recounting of memories of intense experiences, has been an emotionally overwhelming experience that certainly influenced the collected stories. As a result, it was sometimes necessary to stop the interview. Some narrators, especially the younger women's rights activists and human rights defenders, expressed discomfort and unwillingness to go through the experience of narrating, remembering, and reflecting.

An Online Oral History Archive: Issues of Accessibility

In April 2015, WMF launched the Women's Oral History Archive as an online oral history archive (http://oralhistoryarchive.wmf.org.eg). The website features profiles of the narrators with short biographies and abstracts of their interviews. Keywords and a variety of search options guide users in their search. Visually, the website aims to foreground the narrators' images through photos. Some of the profiles include short films (2–4 minutes). Based on the narrators' interviews, these short films show some of the narrators' photos with a voice-over of an excerpt from the oral narrative. The narrators were frequently consulted during the process of filming and editing. Audio files were also included in the narrators' profiles on the website. The audio files allow the website users to hear the voices of the narrators telling their stories. Using different media, such as printed posters, audio recordings, and audio-visual products, helps WMF to reach out to diverse audiences.

With the objective of making feminist knowledge available, accessibility to the materials of the Archive of Women's Oral History has been a priority issue for the team members. How to make the archive available to researchers and the public? Which conditions of availability should be adopted? Should we employ different levels of accessibility? How do we utilize the archive as an advocacy tool?

Modes of accessibility vary between information made available online for advocacy purposes and materials made accessible to researchers only upon request. For example, names of narrators, their bios, and abstracts of their oral narratives are regularly uploaded to the online archive available to the general public. However, the interview transcripts are only accessible at the WMF office upon request. The Archive of Women's Oral History is perceived as an integral part of WMF's other collections of archival materials, photos, personal papers, and memorabilia. Therefore, policies on conditions of availability, and the forms for requesting access, have been developed within a larger context of granting accessibility to all collections housed at WMLDC.

Challenges to Archive Management of Women's Oral History Collections

In addition to the theoretical and practical problems of conducting oral history interviews, other issues have arisen in the course of building and managing a feminist oral history archive on a large scale. As one of the first feminist oral history archives in the Arab region, WMF had to develop strategies and solutions for archival management issues. Our concern has been to devise tools that would reflect feminist and participatory values while being practical and efficient. Therefore, our work has been guided by the literature of feminist approaches to research methodology and oral history, the experiences of relevant oral history archives in other regions in the world, and the feedback we receive from our networks of academics, activists, and researchers. The strategies we adopted have been developed and implemented with many concerns in mind: 1) making feminist knowledge and women's stories accessible to the public, specifically via the online archive; 2) encouraging researchers in the social sciences and humanities to use the archive and facilitating their work; 3) maintaining the voices of the narrators in the transcribed text as well as other printed and multimedia products of the archive; 4) reflecting the values of participatory feminist methodologies in the processes of documentation and dissemination; 5) acknowledging WMF's interventions in the process of documentation, editing, and dissemination in order to maintain transparency and accountability; 6) being aware of issues of power involved in establishing and managing oral history archives in Egypt after 2011; 7) developing sustainable, efficient, and practical solutions that ensure consistency and usability of the archive.

The editorial policy of the WMF archive has been developed and shared on the website. It provides clear guidelines for the various interventions made by the research team in the text of the interview. Most of the interventions have been made with the aim of facilitating the accessibility and readability of the text while maintaining the voices of the narrators. This is a particular challenge because of the gap between oral colloquial Arabic and written standard Arabic. In other cases, the narrators were bilingual and used both Arabic and English during their interviews. While keeping the English words might be important in order to reflect the background and voice of the narrators, using two languages in one text might result in an interrupted flow of the text when read. Hence, the editorial decision was to consistently use one language, particularly since the aim is to make knowledge available to Arabic-speaking audiences.

Moving Forward

More than six years have passed since the first interviews were conducted in spring 2011 to build the Women in the Public Sphere Post-2011 Collection. In late 2015 and early 2016, the work process of the Women's Oral History Archive underwent an assessment where in-depth interviews and focus groups were conducted with narrators, users of the online archive, visitors to the WMLDC, participants in the methodology workshops, and members of the research team. Many of the insights resulting from this assessment, in particular the straightforward ones such as making the website more user-friendly, have already been incorporated within our work.

With a genuine commitment to expand the archive, build new collections, and support the work of feminist documentation in Egypt and across the region, the WMF research team is currently rethinking the aims and direction of the archive. Should we let go of the centrality of the events of the sit-in in Tahrir? Should we focus more on documenting life stories? How can we reflect the diversity of women's experiences?

How can we reflect the changes the narrators experience in their lives and perceptions over the years? How to contextualize the documented oral narrative collections within wider archives? Should we focus more on collecting object materials and memorabilia? And finally, how do we address the challenges of being activist-researchers and activist-documentarians in contemporary Egypt? How can we build a feminist archive that would support movements for social and political change?

References

Anderson, K., and D. C. Jack. 1991. "Learning to Listen: Interview Techniques and Analysis." In S. B. Gluck and D. Patai, eds. *Women's Words: The Feminist Practice of Oral History*, 11–26. New York: Routledge.

Elsadda, H. 2016. "An Archive of Hope: Translating Memories of Revolution." In M. Baker, ed. *Translating Dissent: Voices from and with the Egyptian Revolution*, 148–160. New York: Routledge.

Gluck, S. B., and D. Patai. 1991. "Introduction." In S. B. Gluck and D. Patai, eds. *Women's Words: The Feminist Practice of Oral History*, 1–3. New York: Routledge.

Hayes, P. 2005. "Introduction: Visual Genders," *Gender & History*, 17(3): 519–537.

Hesse-Biber, S. 2013. "Feminist Approaches to In-Depth Interviewing." In S. N. Hesse-Biber, ed. *Handbook of Feminist Research: Theory and Praxis*, 182–232. Los Angeles: SAGE Publications.

CHAPTER 11

University on the Square: Documenting Egypt's 21st-Century Revolution Project

Stephen Urgola

In February 2011, very few people could profess to know with certainty the path that Egypt's "January 25 Revolution" would ultimately take. As with so many others, this was true for members of the University on the Square: Documenting Egypt's 21st-Century Revolution, a project launched at the American University in Cairo (AUC) to preserve a record of the 18 days of protests at Tahrir Square and their aftermath. In the approximately seven years since the project began, its staff needed to adapt to unstable political and technological times, adjusting to new means of documentation and taking into account the shifting political situation of the country.

The project was launched by a group of faculty, staff, and administrators at AUC, coming from a variety of backgrounds such as journalism, political science, library and archives work, and information technology. Besides the professional interests these individuals shared toward the end of documenting developments in Egyptian society, there were other good reasons for the project to come out of AUC. The university's downtown campus buildings on Tahrir Square stood as backdrop to the initial 18 days of protests. More important, many AUC faculty, students, staff, and alumni had participated in the demonstrations and related events. This was opportune for the University on the Square project, which took as its original goal to document the protests through the experiences of the AUC community.

In parallel with the inspiration to document Egypt's changing political scene, project members at the outset were motivated by a concern about the disposition of the evidence and records left behind. They (like others) asked: What would happen with the photos and videos taken on mobile phones, the banners displayed at Tahrir Square, the internet websites, the tear gas canisters picked up as souvenirs? Would this all be preserved for future generations?

AUC had a track record in preserving documentation of the past. Its Rare Books and Special Collections Library, which was to be the repository for the materials collected by University on the Square, is known for the archives of leading figures in Egyptian arts and culture, from architect Hassan Fathy to photographer Van-Leo and artist Salah Taher. Social and political change, especially related to women's roles in Egypt, are documented at the library by collections like that of Hoda Shaarawi. But until 2011, conveying the direct experiences of people who might be called "ordinary Egyptians" had not been a leading concern (nor had it been at many archival institutions). A researcher seeking evidence of citizens' observations about the 1952 Egyptian Revolution in the library's collections would likely have a challenging time. Nor had the library had to deal with the challenge of collecting sheer numbers of items on the scale the January 25 Revolution produced.

As filmmaker Karim El Hakim put it, "I think it (Egypt) was the most photographed revolution in the history of man. You'd have ten people protesting and another fifteen people filming them with their phones" (Halliburton 2012). Beyond depicting the scene at Tahrir Square, El Hakim's statement encapsulated the uncharted waters of the documentary process faced by University on the Square staff, in terms of preserving the record of the revolution produced by ordinary people, in mode and quantity. These were uncertain times, both politically and for documentarians.

And "uncertain" reflected the fate for the material that participants in the demonstrations generated, if it was not specifically targeted and collected by the project. The handwritten signs that so many protesters produced to signal their views drew international attention, in part for their very personal nature in their messages and means of creation. But this kind of material was also so very ephemeral, as such items were generally intended to have no more than a brief lifespan. Project staff, however, realized the value of this kind of 'people's documentation.' But acquiring it meant nearly immediate intervention, in the time between a sign dropping out of a protester's hand to the ground, and being swept up by the trash collectors.

The protests at Tahrir left behind a great deal of historically significant debris that would have disappeared without the efforts of project members. Collecting began early: days after the celebrations of President Mubarak's departure, a project intern gathered up armfuls of banners set up by demonstrators. Some of these signs expressed the general hopes for the revolution, and others reflected the concerns of political parties or interest groups. The continuing demonstrations at Tahrir Square throughout 2011 and 2012—against military rule, about the shape of Egypt's new constitution, and for other reasons—meant continued collecting of what was left behind, often late at night or in the early mornings when the crowds had thinned.

Electoral campaign posters were carried at gatherings as well as pasted on most available wall surfaces in Cairo leading up to the parliamentary and presidential elections in 2011, 2012, and 2013, representing another collecting target for the project. The demonstrations from late 2012 through summer 2013 around Cairo mounted by opponents and supporters of President Muhammad Morsi featured signs and posters reflecting how polarized the country had become.

While the role of internet social media was emphasized in reporting about the revolution, it was sometimes lost in international news reports how much was communicated by traditional channels. Leaflets issued by various parties and interest groups, with a wide variety of messages, were common at the demonstrations in 2011 and 2012, and University on the Square collected a few hundred of these items. Printed newspapers still played a large role in the media landscape in Egypt, so University on the Square staff collected newspapers printed at notable times: protest days, trials of President Mubarak and his sons, at elections, after violent episodes. Filling over forty oversized boxes, these included state and private newspapers, but also journals spanning the range of opinion, including the Freedom and Justice party's newspaper (the latter, and others, have since ceased operations). These materials reveal the shifts in the media coverage and portrayals of Egypt's revolutionary changes.

Beyond signs, banners, and printed media, the project also collected other physical manifestations of the revolution. Donors contributed items related to the protests at Tahrir Square, like tear gas canisters picked up from the ground. Artifacts were also found on the AUC campus, for example a pair of boots belonging to a riot policeman, or hundreds of tear gas canisters and Molotov cocktail devices that had fallen onto the AUC campus during the fighting on Muhammad Mahmud Street in 2012. Souvenirs like flags, hats, wristbands, and stickers (many depicting a license plate reading "Egypt, January 25") were purchased by the project staff from stands at Tahrir Square, Mohandiseen, and elsewhere from early 2011 through 2014.

The souvenirs paint a picture of how politics in Egypt changed during this period. In the first year after January 25, 2011 common items were stickers with satirical cartoons about President Mubarak and his associates, but even more small laminated cards hung from ribbon with images of the martyrs, those young people who lost their lives in the Tahrir protests. Items evoking the ongoing violent clashes between protesters and state authorities, such as goggles and face masks to protect against tear gas, and Guy Fawkes masks often hand-painted in the Egyptian national colors, were acquired at Tahrir Square in 2012. Presidential candidate and then winner Muhammad Morsi became the face of the posters, t-shirts, cards, and other items, until replaced by General (later President) Abd al-Fatah al-Sisi in 2013 and beyond. In the later part of that year and into 2014, yellow stickers featuring the icon of a hand, associated with the dispersal of the Rabaa Square protests, were also acquired for the project.

University on the Square staff addressed the digital evidence of the revolution as well. Despite the ubiquity of digital media, project staff realized that it might be as ephemeral as paper and cardboard signs. Would the many digital photographs and videos taken by participants survive the transfer from mobile telephones or storage on laptop computers or external hard drives? Probably not for long without early acquisition; prospects were dim for a future archivist to benefit from the digital equivalent of finding a stash of letters in a trunk in the basement or box in the attic. For these reasons the project acted quickly on this front, with AUC computing staff developing web modules to allow individuals to upload their digital images and files.

Response to this crowdsourcing method of acquiring photographs and videos was positive, with dozens of donors contributing digital photographs and videos through the University on the Square website.

Assembling documentation in this way, by making a call for wide community participation, took its inspiration from other similar projects in the archives community, especially the Virginia Tech 4-16-07 Archives project that collected and made accessible material related to the mass shooting deaths at that university several years before the 2011 revolution in Egypt. For the Rare Books and Special Collections library, it represented the first time archival material had been acquired in this way.

This methodology underwent change over the life of the project, however. As the 18 days receded and the celebratory mood surrounding the revolution dampened, online submissions dried up. Instead, personal contacts with amateur photographers, or requests for images of people interviewed for oral histories, became the main source. Project staff took photographs themselves, and student staff and volunteers were given photographic assignments, such as capturing images of the extensive street art and graffiti with revolution themes.

The method of providing access to the images represented another new direction, an aspect of the project led by archivists in the Rare Books and Special Collections Library, which had just recently begun making digital resources available online. After trying different platforms, the library made the collected project images available in an online digital library based on the leading remotely-hosted service used in the field of libraries and archives.

The digital aspect of Egypt's 2011 revolution was, of course, highly significant and well known from the outset, given the role of social media websites like the "We are all Khaled Said" Facebook page for mobilizing protesters. Documenting the online activity that paralleled the physical protests was critical to preserving a historical record of what was dubbed in the international media the "Facebook Revolution."

Efforts in this direction began even before University on the Square was launched, with websites related to the protests at Tahrir Square being archived by AUC's Rare Books Library, which had since 2009 used ArchiveIt, a subscription service of the Internet Archive, to preserve websites on a variety of Egypt-oriented topics. A library staff member was in the United States when internet service was cut in Egypt in January 2011, and she used her login to ArchiveIt to begin to capture relevant websites. Since early 2011 the project has archived over five hundred URLs, with links to unique web documents numbering in the millions. These include online news outlets that covered the initial 18 days and events through the present day, blogs and Twitter feeds by activists and others, and the websites of rights organizations, electoral candidates, and activist groups.

A key component of the University on the Square project was the recording of oral history interviews with participants in and observers of the demonstrations, starting with individuals drawn from the AUC community, including students, alumni, staff, faculty, and administrators. The first interviewees were AUC security guards on duty in January 2011, who described the campus being breached by protesters and police. Many AUC community members told their stories of participating in the protests at Tahrir Square, ranging from serious activists, to those curious to observe the scene, to others for whom it was their first foray into political activity. AUC alumni in a variety of fields offered accounts of their involvement as professionals in journalism, politics, and other fields.

Early in the project it became clear that the oral history initiative would be marked by constant change, in parallel with the changes in Egypt's political scene from 2011 to the present. As early as the first month of the project, team members realized that the scope of efforts would have to expand beyond the AUC community to embrace others (often recommended by AUC community members) who had important testimonies to contribute. Thus oral histories were conducted with individuals such as activists who camped in Tahrir Square, faculty and students from Egyptian national universities, football ultras, and even the barber who witnessed events from his shop near the AUC campus. Members of some subcommunities were also represented, like Sudanese refugees who spoke about their experiences while living in Cairo during the revolutionary period. With the reach of interviews growing, there was increasing diversity among those interviewed in terms of the nature of their participation, profession, class, gender, religion, and language. Interviews were conducted in English or Arabic, according to the preference of the interviewee, now about 50 percent in each language.

As developments in political life unfolded in 2011, 2012, and 2013, it became necessary for the oral history team to repeatedly adjust the time frame to be documented. As months of continued protests, elections, and other political developments it grew clear that 'revolution' had to be redefined, and the period of time to be covered had to be extended beyond the initial 18 days. This had practical implications, as project staff had to repeatedly revise the question scripts to reflect contemporary events.

The tone of the interviews also evolved over time, serving as a barometer for the country's political climate. As events played out, the challenge of soliciting interviews mounted, because increasing numbers of potential interviewees became reluctant to be recorded (due to fear of repercussions, depression, or change in their opinion about the revolution); other potential interviewees left Egypt, or died. Thus achieving what could be considered a representative cross-section of opinion has been something of a challenge, in quantitative terms, given the self-selective nature of the interviewees—few supporters of President Mubarak signed up to be interviewed, for example. A breadth of opinion is reflected in the content of the interviews, however. Despite the oftentimes uncertain political situation in Egypt, all interviewees completed and signed oral history agreement forms permitting online access and other usage of their interviews, although the project has made the identity of interviewees anonymous.

Interviews have continued through the present day, however, through the efforts of students (on work-study duty or interviewing as a course assignment), and volunteers who have formed the main corps of oral history interviewers. These interviewers have identified individuals to be interviewed, as have scholars pursuing their own research who donated their completed interviews to the project. Through the end of 2017, University on the Square has built an oral history archive of over 400 interviews, which will ultimately be made available online (audio files, transcripts, and summaries) in the Rare Books Library's digital library.

It seems appropriate that the effort to document changing times in Egypt, the January 25, 2011 revolution and the several years after, take place in an environment of changing documentation methods. These included strategies like collaboration among colleagues from various backgrounds and the use of crowdsourcing to solicit donated material, as well as embracing a variety of media formats and platforms (paper and digital, image and audio) reflecting the events to be recorded. In an unsettled political scene, where even the limits of the events to be documented were uncertain, University on the Square staff had to constantly revisit the way the project was approached and the way material was to be collected and ultimately made available for research. In an era where so many more individuals are able to produce documentation of an event like Egypt's Revolution, whether it be by making a sign, or taking a digital photograph, or lending their voice to an oral history, the project may serve as a model for the new directions in documenting history in changing times.

References

Halliburton, Rachel. 2012. "The Revolution Has Been Photographed," *Prospect Magazine*, July 4. http://www.prospectmagazine.co.uk/blog/the-revolution-will-be-photographed.

About the Contributors

Dr. Faiha Abdulhadi is a writer and founder of Al-Rowat for Studies and Research.

Dr. Hoda Elsadda is professor of English and comparative literature at Cairo University, and co-founder and chair of the Women and Memory Forum.

Dr. Sondra Hale is research professor and professor emerita of anthropology and gender studies at the University of California, Los Angeles.

Dr. Manal Hamzeh is associate professor in the Women's Studies Program at New Mexico State University.

Maissan Hassan is program officer at the Women and Memory Forum.

Dr. Nahawand Elkadery Issa is professor of media studies at the Lebanese University.

Diana Magdy is researcher at the Women and Memory Forum.

Jean Said Makdisi is a novelist and member of the Lebanese Association of Women Researchers (Bahithat).

About the Contributors

Dr. Noor Nieftagodien is NRF chair in Local Histories, Present Realities and head of History Workshop, Wits University, Johannesburg.

Dr. Hanan Sabea is associate professor of anthropology at the American University in Cairo.

Dr. Rafif Saidawy is a novelist and researcher at the Arab Thought Foundation in Beirut.

Dr. Lucine Taminian is associate professor of anthropology at the American University of Beirut.

Stephen Urgola is university archivist and director of records management at the Rare Books and Special Collections Library, the American University in Cairo.

CAIRO PAPERS IN SOCIAL SCIENCE

Volume One
1   *Women, Health and Development,* Cynthia Nelson, ed.
2   *Democracy in Egypt,* Ali E. Hillal Dessouki, ed.
3   *Mass Communications and the October War,* Olfat Hassan Agha
4   *Rural Resettlement in Egypt,* Helmy Tadros
5   *Saudi Arabian Bedouin,* Saad E. Ibrahim and Donald P. Cole

Volume Two
1   *Coping with Poverty in a Cairo Community,* Andrea B. Rugh
2   *Modernization of Labor in the Arab Gulf,* Enid Hill
3   *Studies in Egyptian Political Economy,* Herbert M. Thompson
4   *Law and Social Change in Contemporary Egypt,* Cynthia Nelson and Klaus Friedrich Koch, eds.
5   *The Brain Drain in Egypt,* Saneya Saleh

Volume Three
1   *Party and Peasant in Syria,* Raymond Hinnebusch
2   *Child Development in Egypt,* Nicholas V. Ciaccio
3   *Living without Water,* Asaad Nadim et al.
4   *Export of Egyptian School Teachers,* Suzanne A. Messiha
5   *Population and Urbanization in Morocco,* Saad E. Ibrahim

Volume Four
1   *Cairo's Nubian Families,* Peter Geiser
2, 3   *Symposium on Social Research for Development: Proceedings,* Social Research Center
4   *Women and Work in the Arab World,* Earl L. Sullivan and Karima Korayem

Volume Five
1   *Ghagar of Sett Guiranha: A Study of a Gypsy Community in Egypt,* Nabil Sobhi Hanna
2   *Distribution of Disposal Income and the Impact of Eliminating Food Subsidies in Egypt,* Karima Korayem
3   *Income Distribution and Basic Needs in Urban Egypt,* Amr Mohie el-Din

Volume Six
1 *The Political Economy of Revolutionary Iran*, Mihssen Kadhim
2 *Urban Research Strategies in Egypt*, Richard A. Lobban, ed.
3 *Non-alignment in a Changing World*, Mohammed el-Sayed Selim, ed.
4 *The Nationalization of Arabic and Islamic Education in Egypt: Dar al-Alum and al-Azhar*, Lois A. Arioan

Volume Seven
1 *Social Security and the Family in Egypt*, Helmi Tadros
2 *Basic Needs, Inflation and the Poor of Egypt*, Myrette el-Sokkary
3 *The Impact of Development Assistance on Egypt*, Earl L. Sullivan, ed.
4 *Irrigation and Society in Rural Egypt*, Sohair Mehanna, Richard Huntington, and Rachad Antonius

Volume Eight
1, 2 *Analytic Index of Survey Research in Egypt*, Madiha el-Safty, Monte Palmer, and Mark Kennedy

Volume Nine
1 *Philosophy, Ethics and Virtuous Rule*, Charles E. Butterworth
2 *The 'Jihad': An Islamic Alternative in Egypt*, Nemat Guenena
3 *The Institutionalization of Palestinian Identity in Egypt*, Maha A. Dajani
4 *Social Identity and Class in a Cairo Neighborhood*, Nadia A. Taher

Volume Ten
1 *Al-Sanhuri and Islamic Law*, Enid Hill
2 *Gone for Good*, Ralph Sell
3 *The Changing Image of Women in Rural Egypt*, Mona Abaza
4 *Informal Communities in Cairo: the Basis of a Typology*, Linda Oldham, Haguer el Hadidi, and Hussein Tamaa

Volume Eleven
1 *Participation and Community in Egyptian New Lands: The Case of South Tahrir*, Nicholas Hopkins et al.
2 *Palestinian Universities under Occupation*, Antony T. Sullivan
3 *Legislating Infitah: Investment, Foreign Trade and Currency Laws*, Khaled M. Fahmy
4 *Social History of an Agrarian Reform Community in Egypt*, Reem Saad

Volume Twelve
1 *Cairo's Leap Forward: People, Households, and Dwelling Space*, Fredric Shorter
2 *Women, Water, and Sanitation: Household Water Use in Two Egyptian Villages*, Samiha el-Katsha et al.
3 *Palestinian Labor in a Dependent Economy: Women Workers in the West Bank Clothing Industry*, Randa Siniora
4 *The Oil Question in Egyptian–Israeli Relations, 1967–1979: A Study in International Law and Resource Politics*, Karim Wissa

Volume Thirteen
1 *Squatter Markets in Cairo*, Helmi R. Tadros, Mohamed Feteeha, and Allen Hibbard
2 *The Sub-culture of Hashish Users in Egypt: A Descriptive Analytic Study*, Nashaat Hassan Hussein
3 *Social Background and Bureaucratic Behavior in Egypt*, Earl L. Sullivan, el Sayed Yassin, Ali Leila, and Monte Palmer
4 *Privatization: The Egyptian Debate*, Mostafa Kamel el-Sayyid

Volume Fourteen
1 *Perspectives on the Gulf Crisis*, Dan Tschirgi and Bassam Tibi
2 *Experience and Expression: Life among Bedouin Women in South Sinai*, Deborah Wickering
3 *Impact of Temporary International Migration on Rural Egypt*, Atef Hanna Nada
4 *Informal Sector in Egypt*, Nicholas S. Hopkins, ed.

Volume Fifteen
1 *Scenes of Schooling: Inside a Girls' School in Cairo*, Linda Herrera
2 *Urban Refugees: Ethiopians and Eritreans in Cairo*, Dereck Cooper
3 *Investors and Workers in the Western Desert of Egypt: An Exploratory Survey*, Naeim Sherbiny, Donald Cole, and Nadia Makary
4 *Environmental Challenges in Egypt and the World*, Nicholas S. Hopkins, ed.

Volume Sixteen
1 *The Socialist Labor Party: A Case Study of a Contemporary Egyptian Opposition Party*, Hanaa Fikry Singer
2 *The Empowerment of Women: Water and Sanitation Initiatives in Rural Egypt*, Samiha el Katsha and Susan Watts
3 *The Economics and Politics of Structural Adjustment in Egypt: Third Annual Symposium*

4 *Experiments in Community Development in a Zabbaleen Settlement*, Marie Assaad and Nadra Garas

Volume Seventeen
1 *Democratization in Rural Egypt: A Study of the Village Local Popular Council*, Hanan Hamdy Radwan
2 *Farmers and Merchants: Background for Structural Adjustment in Egypt*, Sohair Mehanna, Nicholas S. Hopkins, and Bahgat Abdelmaksoud
3 *Human Rights: Egypt and the Arab World, Fourth Annual Symposium*
4 *Environmental Threats in Egypt: Perceptions and Actions*, Salwa S. Gomaa, ed.

Volume Eighteen
1 *Social Policy in the Arab World*, Jacqueline Ismael and Tareq Y. Ismael
2 *Workers, Trade Unions and the State in Egypt: 1984–1989*, Omar el-Shafie
3 *The Development of Social Science in Egypt: Economics, History and Sociology; Fifth Annual Symposium*
4 *Structural Adjustment, Stabilization Policies and the Poor in Egypt*, Karima Korayem

Volume Nineteen
1 *Nilopolitics: A Hydrological Regime, 1870–1990*, Mohamed Hatem el-Atawy
2 *Images of the Other: Europe and the Muslim World before 1700*, David R. Blanks et al.
3 *Grass Roots Participation in the Development of Egypt*, Saad Eddin Ibrahim et al.
4 *The Zabbalin Community of Muqattam*, Elena Volpi and Doaa Abdel Motaal

Volume Twenty
1 *Class, Family, and Power in an Egyptian Village*, Samer el-Karanshawy
2 *The Middle East and Development in a Changing World*, Donald Heisel, ed.
3 *Arab Regional Women's Studies Workshop*, Cynthia Nelson and Soraya Altorki, eds.
4 *"Just a Gaze": Female Clientele of Diet Clinics in Cairo: An Ethnomedical Study*, Iman Farid Bassyouny

Volume Twenty-one
1 *Turkish Foreign Policy during the Gulf War of 1990–1991*, Mostafa Aydin
2 *State and Industrial Capitalism in Egypt*, Samer Soliman
3 *Twenty Years of Development in Egypt (1977–1997): Part I*, Mark C. Kennedy

4   *Twenty Years of Development in Egypt (1977–1997): Part II,* Mark C. Kennedy

Volume Twenty-two
1   *Poverty and Poverty Alleviation Strategies in Egypt,* Ragui Assaad and Malak Rouchdy
2   *Between Field and Text: Emerging Voices in Egyptian Social Science,* Seteney Shami and Linda Hererra, eds.
3   *Masters of the Trade: Crafts and Craftspeople in Cairo, 1750–1850,* Pascale Ghazaleh
4   *Discourses in Contemporary Egypt: Politics and Social Issues,* Enid Hill, ed.

Volume Twenty-three
1   *Fiscal Policy Measures in Egypt: Public Debt and Food Subsidy,* Gouda Abdel-Khalek and Karima Korayem
2   *New Frontiers in the Social History of the Middle East,* Enid Hill, ed.
3   *Egyptian Encounters,* Jason Thompson, ed.
4   *Women's Perception of Environmental Change in Egypt,* Eman el Ramly

Volume Twenty-four
1, 2   *The New Arab Family,* Nicholas S. Hopkins, ed.
3   *An Investigation of the Phenomenon of Polygyny in Rural Egypt,* Laila S. Shahd
4   *The Terms of Empowerment: Islamic Women Activists in Egypt,* Sherine Hafez

Volume Twenty-five
1, 2   *Elections in the Middle East: What Do They Mean?* Iman A. Hamdy, ed.
3   *Employment Crisis of Female Graduates in Egypt: An Ethnographic Account,* Ghada F. Barsoum
4   *Palestinian and Israeli Nationalism: Identity Politics and Education in Jerusalem,* Evan S. Weiss

Volume Twenty-six
1   *Culture and Natural Environment: Ancient and Modern Middle Eastern Texts,* Sharif S. Elmusa, ed.
2   *Street Children in Egypt: Group Dynamics and Subcultural Constituents,* Nashaat Hussein
3   *IMF–Egyptian Debt Negotiations,* Bessma Momani
4   *Forced Migrants and Host Societies in Egypt and Sudan,* Fabienne Le Houérou

Volume Twenty-seven
1, 2 *Cultural Dynamics in Contemporary Egypt*, Maha Abdelrahman, Iman A. Hamdy, Malak Rouchdy, and Reem Saad, eds.
3 *The Role of Local Councils in Empowerment and Poverty Reduction*, Solava Ibrahim
4 *Beach Politics: Gender and Sexuality in Dahab*, Mustafa Abdalla

Volume Twenty-eight
1 *Creating Families across Boundaries: A Case Study of Romanian/Egyptian Mixed Marriages*, Ana Vinea
2, 3 *Pioneering Feminist Anthropology in Egypt: Selected Writings from Cynthia Nelson*, Martina Rieker, ed.
4 *Roses in Salty Soil: Women and Depression in Egypt Today*, Dalia A. Mostafa

Volume Twenty-nine
1 *Crossing Borders, Shifting Boundaries: Palestinian Dilemmas*, Sari Hanafi, ed.
2, 3 *Political and Social Protest in Egypt*, Nicholas S. Hopkins, ed.
4 *The Experience of Protest: Masculinity and Agency among Sudanese Refugees in Cairo*, Martin T. Rowe

Volume Thirty
1 *Child Protection Policies in Egypt: A Rights-Based Approach*, Adel Azer, Sohair Mehanna, Mulki Al-Sharmani, and Essam Ali
2 *"The Farthest Place": Social Boundaries in an Egyptian Desert Community*, Joseph Viscomi
3 *The New York Egyptians: Voyages and Dreams*, Yasmine M. Ahmed
4 *The Burden of Resources: Oil and Water in the Gulf and the Nile Basin*, Sharif S. Elmusa, ed.

Volume Thirty-one
1 *Humanist Perspectives on Sacred Space*, David Blanks, Bradley S. Clough, eds.
2 *Law as a Tool for Empowering Women within Marital Relations: A Case Study of Paternity Lawsuits in Egypt*, Hind Ahmed Zaki
3,4 *Visual Productions of Knowledge: Toward a Different Middle East*, Hanan Sabea, Mark R. Westmoreland, eds.

Volume Thirty-two
1 *Planning Egypt's New Settlements: The Politics of Spatial Inequities*, Dalia Wahdan

2   *Agrarian Transformation in the Arab World: Persistent and Emerging Challenges*, Habib Ayeb and Reem Saad
3   *Femininity and Dance in Egypt: Embodiment and Meaning in al-Raqs al-Baladi*, Noha Roushdy
4   *Negotiating Space: The Evolution of the Egyptian Street, 2000–2011*, Dimitris Soudias

Volume Thirty-three
1   *Masculinities in Egypt and the Arab World: Historical, Literary, and Social Science Perspectives*, Helen Rizzo, ed.
2   *Anthropology in Egypt 1900–1967: Culture, Function, and Reform*, Nicholas S. Hopkins
3   *The Church in the Square: Negotiations of Religion and Revolution at an Evangelical Church in Cairo*, Anna Jeannine Dowell
4   *The Political Economy of the New Egyptian Republic*, Nicholas S. Hopkins, ed.

Volume Thirty-four
1   *Egyptian Hip-Hop: Expressions from the Underground*, Ellen R. Weis
2   *Sports and Society in the Middle East*, Nicholas S. Hopkins and Sandrine Gamblin, eds.
3   *Organizing the Unorganized: Migrant Domestic Workers in Lebanon*, Farah Kobaissy
4   *The Food Question in the Middle East*, Malak S. Rouchdy and Iman A. Hamdy, eds.

www.ingramcontent.com/pod-product-compliance
Lightning Source LLC
Chambersburg PA
CBHW071919070526
44583CB00016B/2052